129 BIRDS IN FULL COLOR

BIRDS

A GUIDE TO FAMILIAR BIRDS
OF NORTH AMERICA

a Golden Guide® from St. Martin's Press

by
HERBERT S. ZIM
and
IRA N. GABRIELSON

Revised by
CHANDLER S. ROBBINS

Updated by
JONATHAN P. LATIMER
and
KAREN STRAY NOLTING
with
JAMES COE

Illustrated by
JAMES GORDON IRVING

St. Martin's Press   New York

FOREWORD

For more than a generation this book, along with other Golden Guides, has introduced thousands of children and adults to the diversity of the natural world. It has helped to increase people's awareness of the environment and to share the pleasure of learning and understanding about the lives of birds. This guide illustrates 129 of the most familiar varieties, and the text gives concise information to help identify each one. The text also discusses similar species, helping the reader to identify more than 250 birds in all. This revision reflects the latest information on birds, including recent changes in bird classification and common and scientific names.

The birds in this book were carefully selected through detailed study of the voluminous data available about bird life. This study relied on the cooperation and assistance of the many experts who contributed to the original edition. John Aldrich, C. C. Cottam, Allen Duvall, D. F. Hoffmeister, A. C. Martin, Ernst Mayr, A. L. Nelson, A. Sprunt, IV, R. E. Stewart, H. L. Webster, and Alex Wetmore gave helpful comments and suggestions. Special thanks go to Chandler S. Robbins of the Patuxent Wildlife Research Center, one of the great pioneers in birding. He compiled the original data for the range maps and other factual information in the book, and edited the previous revision. Special thanks also go to Herbert S. Zim who conceived Golden Guides and did so much to nurture their growth.

J. P. L.
K. S. N.

ISBN 1-58238-128-3

HOW TO USE THIS BOOK

This field guide is designed to make identifying common birds quick and easy. It can be taken along when you go looking for birds. Don't hesitate to write in this book. It can become a useful record of what you see.

Illustrations The birds illustrated in this guide are among the most common. In almost every part of the United States and southern Canada you can see many of the birds in this book. The color plates show the spring plumage of adult male birds. Females and young are also shown if they are very different.

Text The text emphasizes size, identifying marks, important facts, differences between males and females, and related birds that are similar. The birds have been selected so that knowing one bird will help you to know others like it.

Maps The description of each bird in this guide is accompanied by a map showing where that bird is most likely to be seen.
- Red areas show where birds live in summer.
- Blue indicates winter areas.
- Purple shows where the bird is a permanent resident.

Check each range map for birds that occur in your region. You can learn local birds quickly if you concentrate on these birds, but remember that migrating birds pass over parts of the white areas in spring and fall. Also look at their "timetable" in the chart on pages 132–153, where you will also find information on nests, eggs, and food.

HOW TO IDENTIFY BIRDS

While some kinds of guides are arranged by color, bird guides are generally organized so that closely related species—those of similar shape and behavior—are together. Water birds appear first, followed by more primitive land birds; the true songbirds are last.

You will quickly learn to sort unknown birds into major categories (called orders) such as herons, ducks, hawks, woodpeckers, and perching birds (see pages 9–11). For water birds, note whether they wade, swim, or dive; for aerial feeders whether they constantly flap, soar, or hover. For all birds, look closely at the size and shape of their bill (pages 14–15) and the shape and length of their tail. Compare the total length with that of some familiar species. Is it the size of a sparrow, a robin, or a crow? These characteristics will help place birds in the correct family.

Field Marks   The next step is to determine the species by looking for the presence or absence of wing bars, tail patterns, eye rings or eye stripes, and color patterns on the head or elsewhere. Is the back plain or streaked? Do the underparts have horizontal bars or longitudinal streaks?

Behavior   How a bird acts can also provide valuable clues. Does it walk or hop or run? Does it wag its tail? Does it catch insects on the wing like a swift or a swallow? Or does it repeatedly return to an exposed perch to eat insect prey like a flycatcher or a waxwing? Does it climb up a tree trunk like a woodpecker or climb head-down like a nuthatch? Does it eat berries like a thrush or an oriole, or probe in the ground for worms and grubs like a robin, blackbird, or starling? As a help, the principal foods of each species are listed on pages 132–153.

EQUIPMENT   There are ways to increase your enjoyment of birding—none of which involves much expense. This book is one way, for a guide book is an important tool. As you acquire experience, you will want more advanced books (see page 154). Rugged clothing, waterproof boots, and mosquito repellent are part of an experienced birder's equipment.

Life List   Many people keep a list of all the species they have seen, which is known as a life list. A pocket notebook will help you record detailed information, including the date and place you saw a bird. Over time this list will become a valuable tool for reminding you of what you have seen.

Binoculars   This is the most important and most expensive item of equipment. A good pair of binoculars is a precision tool and should be selected with care. The best glasses are made with prisms to reduce their size and weight. Weight is an important consideration because you will want to be able to hold your binoculars steady or wear them around your neck for long periods of time.

The power of the glass tells you how much closer it will make a bird appear. Seen through 6x (6-power) glasses, a bird looks six times as close. Glasses of 6x to 8x are best. Remember, the higher the power, the more limited your field of vision. Glasses that admit the most light are also best. This depends on the width of the front lens (usually measured in millimeters). A 6 x 35 lens admits twice as much light as a 6 x 24. Lightweight 7 x 35 or 8 x 42 binoculars are excellent for birding. Some birders use 10 x 50 binoculars, but they tend to be heavy.

Be sure to carefully test a pair of binoculars before you make your purchase. You'll want a comfortable pair that you can focus quickly.

WHERE TO LOOK   Birds are everywhere, but to see the most birds try looking in the best places—in moist woodlands or perhaps at the edge of a wooded swamp. Young scrubby woods are likely to have more birds than mature forests. Wood margins are generally good, especially during migration. But no single place is best. Saltwater marshes and shores will yield birds that one will never see in pine woods. Other species prefer open fields, or western deserts. A wooded park in the midst of a city is one of the very best places to look for birds during migration. If you explore your region, you will discover certain spots are favored—perhaps a small glen with a brook, a wooded point on a lake, or trees along a river. On page 155 is a list of some famous places to see birds. Make local inquiries. See also the books and museums and zoos listed on page 154.

HOW TO LOOK   Experienced watchers go out early in the morning when birds are most active. They will often sit quietly in a likely spot and let the birds come to them. Keen-eyed birds are easily frightened by movement. Don't make yourself conspicuous against open sky. Move slowly. Try to cover several distinct habitats, if possible—a woodland, marsh, field, river bank, shore, or whatever your locality affords. Eventually you will work out a route that will give you the greatest variety of birds per time spent. Experience in your own region will be your best help. Make bird watching a year-round activity, for each season has its own special surprises and delights to offer the careful observer.

WHY LOOK?   Birds are by far the most popular of wildlife because they are easy to see, easy to identify, beautiful to observe, attractive to hear, and ever changing in occurrence and numbers. They can also be surprising. Many species migrate long distances, and at times large numbers of birds are blown off course and discovered hundreds of miles from their usual homes.

Birds are indicators of the health of the environment. Changes in their numbers, the appearance of an unusual or unexpected species, or the disappearance of a familiar one can tell us much about changes in the condition of the natural world. Birds have become the focus of local, national, and international conservation efforts, leading to the establishment of preserves, reclamation of wild lands, and protection of flyways and nesting areas.

Some birders prefer to do their observing by themselves, others prefer the sociability of birding in a small group. Many enjoy competition, such as finding more species than a friend or being the first to spot a returning migrant. There are hundreds of bird clubs you can join in the United States and Canada. Thousands of people take bird tours to exotic places. Others keep impressive lists of the species they have seen. Even a simple bird feeder or birdbath can bring much pleasure right at home.

An interest in birds can be enjoyed throughout life and can give pleasure at any place and at any time. It often expands into a greater appreciation for all wildlife, and for the habitats that are essential to its survival.

PARTS OF A BIRD

Bird experts have dozens of technical names for the various parts of birds. Using these terms, they can describe a bird with great accuracy. A beginner does not have the experience to use these terms, so only the essential technical terms are used in this book. When you see a bird you cannot identify, try to observe the bird as well as you can. Study its size, habits, and the color and form of the parts illustrated above. Put your information down on paper (don't trust your memory). By keeping these few parts in mind you will systematize your observations and record the details needed to get your bird identified.

BIRD CLASSIFICATION

Birds are grouped into orders, families, and genera according to similarities in their bills, feet, and internal anatomy. This simplified list of the bird groups in this book will help you understand how they are classified and what to look for. The scientific name of each bird in this guide is listed on pages 156–157. Those names and the English names used have been adopted by the American Ornithologists' Union (AOU).

LOONS Large swimming and diving birds with short tails, legs set far back, and sharply pointed bills. They often float with only their head above water. **page 21**

GREBES Smaller swimmers and divers. Tail lacking; legs set far back; bill slender and pointed. They dive by thrusting their head down, disappearing without a ripple. **page 22**

HERONS, BITTERNS, and EGRETS Long-legged wading birds with long necks and straight pointed bills. In flight, their feet extend beyond their tail but their neck is pulled in. They are often seen wading or walking along a shore. **pages 23–25**

DUCKS, GEESE, and SWANS Swimming birds with distinct tails. They walk well compared to grebes or loons. Feet have four toes with the front three webbed. Bill broad and flat. Often found in large flocks. **pages 26–33**

RAILS and COOTS Marsh birds that fly with their neck extended and feet dangling (rails); wings rounded. Feet are unwebbed, except for coot's, which has lobes (see illus. on page 15). Rails usually hunt alone in dense marsh grasses. Coots often gather in large flocks on open water. **page 34**

PLOVERS and SANDPIPERS Long-legged shorebirds, mostly small. Although their silhouettes are similar, plovers are considered a separate family from sandpipers. Plovers are often found on open ground, darting about in a stop-and-go fashion. Sandpipers are found along shores. They probe for food in the mud with their bills. **pages 35–39**

GULLS and TERNS Mostly light-colored marine birds with long, pointed wings. They are often found in noisy flocks, usually near water. Terns are smaller and more slender than gulls, and fly more gracefully. **pages 40–41**

VULTURES, EAGLES, and HAWKS Large birds with strong hooked bills and powerful curved talons. Vultures are scavengers with bare heads. They often are seen in flocks. Eagles and hawks are hunters that are usually seen alone. **pages 42–47**

GROUSE, QUAIL, and TURKEY Plump, chicken-like birds that scratch for food. Their bills are short and stout, their feet heavy and strong, and their wings short and rounded. They spend most of their time on the ground, but may fly up into trees when alarmed. **pages 48–50**

PIGEONS and DOVES Small-headed birds with short bills, stout bodies, and short legs. They feed on seeds and grain on the ground, but some also eat fruit. All are very fast fliers. **pages 51–52**

CUCKOOS Long, slim birds with slightly curved bill and long tail. Most hide in dense foliage. **page 53**

OWLS Although their shapes and behavior are similar, owls are now divided into two families: Barn Owls and Typical Owls. Both have strongly hooked bills, large curved claws, and soft feathers that allow them to fly almost completely silently at night.
pages 54–56

SWIFTS Small swallow-like birds with streamlined bodies and long, slender wings. They are fast fliers and seldom land, feeding on insects caught in flight. **page 57**

NIGHTHAWKS and NIGHTJARS With large heads, small bills, and wide mouths, they scoop insects out of the air. They usually hunt at night and roost on the ground during the day. **pages 58–59**

HUMMINGBIRDS Tiny birds with slender, needle-like bills. Their rapid wing beats allow them to hover and even fly backwards. Their feathers often shine brilliantly.
page 60

KINGFISHERS With large heads, long, pointed bills, and small feet, kingfishers often hover over water, then plunge head-first to catch fish. They also perch above water.
page 61

WOODPECKERS Climbing birds with strong, pointed bills, and stiff, pointed tail feathers. They creep up the sides of trees and pound on bark for their food. **pages 62–65**

PERCHING BIRDS The largest bird group (also known as passerines), accounting for almost 60 percent of all birds. All are land birds adapted for perching on small branches or twigs. Many sing. **pages 66–127**

Vultures

Pelicans

Loons

Petrels and Kin

Storks

Flamingo

Ibis

Herons

Boobies

Anhinga

Cormorants

Nuthatches

Tropicbirds

Gulls and Terns

Grebes

Falcons

Plovers

Sandpipers

Jacana

Cranes

Limpkin

Coots and Rails

Waterfowl

Pigeons

Quails and Kin

Parrots

A FAMILY TREE OF BIRDS

The over 900 species of birds seen in North America north of Mexico are classified into around 70 families. The major families and their approximate relationships are shown here. Families with the most species north of Mexico are represented by the thickest branches.

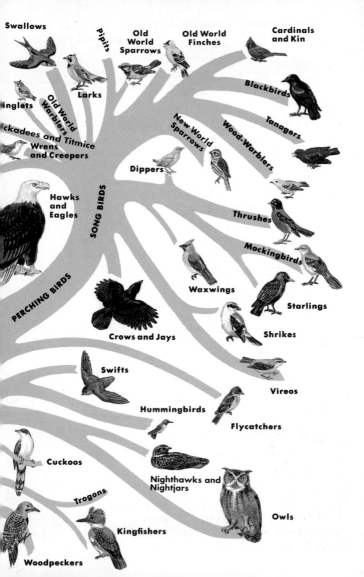

Swallows

pipits

Old World Sparrows

Old World Finches

Cardinals and Kin

Larks

Blackbirds

Old World Warblers

New World Sparrows

Wood-Warblers

Tanagers

inglets

ickadees and Titmice

Wrens and Creepers

Dippers

SONG BIRDS

Thrushes

Hawks and Eagles

Mockingbirds

Waxwings

Starlings

PERCHING BIRDS

Crows and Jays

Shrikes

Swifts

Vireos

Hummingbirds

Flycatchers

Cuckoos

Nighthawks and Nightjars

Trogons

Owls

Kingfishers

Woodpeckers

Tern   Loon   Heron   Kingfisher

ADAPTATIONS OF BIRDS

ADAPTATIONS

Birds show unusual adaptations to their way of life. The most important and obvious is their covering of feathers which developed from the scaly covering of reptiles or dinosaurs. Each feather has rows of branched barbs that hook together. On long flight feathers, these barbs mesh tightly to form a firm structure. Contour feathers and an undercoat of finer feathers cover a bird's body. The form and structure of feathers vary with different birds.

Internal adaptations of birds include air sacs and light, hollow bones that are an advantage for flying. A rapid heartbeat and high body temperature (several degrees higher than ours) favor a very active existence. The animal food birds eat includes insects, worms, mollusks, fish, and small mammals. Plant foods include seeds, buds, leaves, and fruits. The bills of different birds show obvious adaptations related to diet. The four birds shown above, each from a different family, have similar bills adapted for eating fish.

Robin-perching

Ptarmigan-feathered

Pheasant-walking

Duck-swimming

Primary Flight Feather

Barbs and barbules enlarged

vane   shaft   quill

Shrike · Cardinal · Wood Thrush · Crossbill · Yellowthroat

OF FEET

Owl—
grasping

Woodpecker
—climbing

Yellowlegs
—wading

Coot—
swimming

The five birds above all come from a common ancestor and belong to the same order—perching birds (or passerines). But each of these species has developed a different type of bill suited for eating different foods. This type of divergent development is found in many species.

Other adaptations are found in the legs and feet of birds. A bird's three or four toes have been modified for climbing, scratching, grasping and tearing, or swimming. Long toes distribute the weight of birds that walk on mud and sand. Extra feathering protects the feet of ptarmigans and owls that live in the Arctic. The long legs of waders, the webbed feet of swimmers, and other adaptations indicate specialized uses of various kinds.

Most interesting of all adaptations are those of behavior. Many species have developed distinct patterns of living. As you watch, you will discover the "personalities" of different birds and their social adaptations.

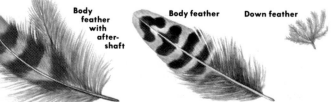

Body feather with aftershaft · Body feather · Down feather

ATTRACTING BIRDS

Lewis's Woodpecker at feeding station

Most of us start watching birds close to home, at a window or in our backyard. One way to see more birds is to make your home more attractive to them. The key is to provide the basic necessities for birds: food, water, and shelter.

FEEDING BIRDS   If you want to attract birds to your yard or window, then feeding them will help. Many places sell bird seed and bird feeders, but even scattering seed on the ground will attract some species. Black-oil sunflower seed is one of the best choices because it is eaten by so many different birds: cardinals, jays, chickadees, finches, even woodpeckers. Seed mixes that include hemp, millet, thistle (Niger) seed, or cracked corn also work.

Downy Woodpeckers like suet

Bird feeders come in many shapes and sizes but it's best to start simply. Birds will come to a raised platform or window shelf, but a tube feeder or hopper feeder need to be replenished less often. During winter you can place lumps of suet in a wire container outside. It will attract chickadees, nuthatches, and woodpeckers. Try replacing the suet with a sandwich made with peanut butter, especially during warmer months. When they find it, your birds will come back to it.

Siskins and other finches enjoy sunflower and thistle seeds

WATER FOR BIRDS Birds need drinking and bathing water just as much as they need food. They are attracted to moving, shallow water. A dripping hose or a trickle of water running into a one-inch pan with gravel on the bottom is excellent. An old bucket with a triangular piece of cloth pulled through a drip hole and hung over an old baking pan will do as well as an elaborate pool.

Drip-bucket provides water

COVER AND SHELTER Birds need cover for protection against wind, cold, and their enemies. The best kind of cover is shrubs or vines that provide food as well as a place to hide. Make sure that there is some place to hide near your bird feeders. Predators are sometimes attracted to the commotion at a feeder and your birds will need a safe place to fly to.

Martin box

Plants for birds can be added to any garden. These include shrubs, such as sumac and boxwood, and small trees, such as holly or dogwood. Shrubs and trees that produce berries or fruits,

Wren house

Wood Duck house

such as cherry, crab apple, or hawthorn, are also good, but native plants that retain their fruit in winter are best. Evergreens may be planted for shelter. Annual flowers such as sunflower, marigold, and zinnia produce seed that attract birds, as do perennials such as aster and black-eyed Susan.

NESTING BOXES   Some birds will take advantage of a nesting box or bird house made by humans. But different boxes will attract different species. For example, a box made for a wren is very different from one made for a flicker. Bird houses and plans for bird houses come in hundreds of different sizes and types. When you have become familiar with the birds in your area, you can choose the right one for those species. Build or buy a box that can be used year after year. Don't place boxes too close together; three or four nesting boxes to an acre are usually enough. Most birds set up their own territory and will keep other birds away.

BIRD PHOTOGRAPHY   Photographing a bird calls for patience and skill, but one fine shot makes it all worthwhile. Try focusing on a bird feeder for a start. Use a camera with a fast lens. A flash is usually necessary for close photos even in daylight.

Steller's Jay (11 in.), only crested jay of the western conifers

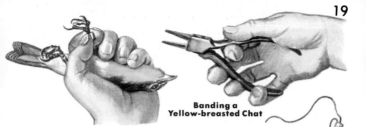

**Banding a
Yellow-breasted Chat**

BIRD BANDING Lightweight aluminum or plastic bands are put around birds' legs by many organizations to help in scientific studies. It doesn't hurt the bird, but much of what we know about migration, flyways, life spans, and population changes has been learned from banded birds. More than a million birds are banded each year.

Bird banding takes place in almost every part of North America, and most groups use volunteers to help. If you are interested, you can find out more through your local birding club. If you find a sick or dead bird with an aluminum band (except a pigeon), look for an 8 or 9 digit number on the band. It may also have a message that reads "CALL 1-800-327-BAND and WRITE BIRD BAND LAUREL MD 20708 USA" or "AVISE BIRD BAND WASH DC." These bands can be reported by calling toll-free 1-800-327-BAND (2263) or by writing to the Bird Banding Laboratory, USGS Patuxent Wildlife Research Center, 12100 Beech Forest Road, Laurel, MD 20708-4039 (http://www.pwrc.usgs.gov/). In either case, you should provide the band number and how, when, and where the bird or band was found.

Color bands

Official bird bands

ADVISE FISH & WILDLIFE SERVICE
WRITE   WASHINGTON DC. USA.
509·12168

BIRD COUNTS Counting birds helps us understand more about migrations and changes in their populations. The best-known count takes place each year during the Christmas season. More than 50,000 birders count birds all over North America during a single 24-hour period. To participate in a Christmas Bird Count, contact a local bird club or write to the National Audubon Society, 700 Broadway, New York, NY 10003. Another count, the North American Migrations Count (NAMC), is held each year on the second Saturday in May. Local coordinators can be found in nearly every county, but you can learn more by writing the NAMC Coordinator, PO Box 71, North Beach, MD 20714.

BREEDING BIRD ATLASES In many states and provinces, intensive mapping projects are in progress to show the nesting range of every bird species. Each state is divided into squares of about 10 square miles each. Volunteers compile lists of birds found in each square during the nesting season. These atlas projects usually take five years to complete. They are repeated after a period of years to find out what changes in bird distribution have occurred. To find out whether an Atlas project is in progress in your area, contact the Cornell Laboratory of Ornithology, 159 Sapsucker Woods Road, Ithaca, NY 14850, 1-800-843-BIRD (2473). The Lab also sponsors Project FeederWatch in which people report what kinds of birds visit their feeders each week, and Project Pigeon-Watch which reports on pigeon flocks in cities.

OTHER VOLUNTEER ACTIVITIES Many other opportunities are available for interested birders. A *Guide to Volunteer Opportunities for Birders* can be obtained from the American Birding Association, PO Box 6599, Colorado Springs, CO 80934. You can also contact the American Ornithologists' Union (AOU), c/o Division of Birds, National Museum of Natural History, Washington, D.C. 20560.

COMMON LOON Spot loons by their large size, long body, short neck, pointed bill, and loud, yodel-like call. Loons are expert divers, but kick along the water before taking flight. In winter, Common Loon (24 in.) is gray above and white beneath. The Red-throated Loon (17 in.) and Pacific Loon (18 in.), both much smaller birds with slender bills, are distinguished by a red or black throat patch, contrasting with a gray head.

PIED-BILLED GREBE Grebes are expert divers and swimmers. Smaller than most ducks, they float lower in the water, and are rarely seen in flight. The Pied-billed Grebe (9 in.) has a more rounded bill than other grebes. The throat patch is lacking in winter. The Horned Grebe

(9½ in.) is told in summer by black head with bright chestnut ear patches. Red-necked Grebe (13 in.) is grayer, with conspicuous white cheek patches and a long, pointed, yellowish bill.

GREAT BLUE HERON, our largest dark-colored wader, flies with a slow, regular wing beat. It usually nests in colonies. It gives a series of low-pitched croaks when flushed. Told from other herons by its size (38 in.). The slender-billed Tricolored Heron (22 in.) of southern coastal marshes has a sharply contrasting white belly. The short-necked, short-legged adult Black-crowned Night-Heron (21 in.) is pale grayish with a black back and black cap; young are streaked brown and white.

GREEN HERON   This small solitary heron (14 in.) is scarcely larger than a crow. It has a typical heron flight, with slow, deep wing strokes. Like other herons it eats aquatic animals. At a distance it may be confused with the larger American Bittern (23 in.) or an immature night-heron (21 in.), but its body is unstreaked and its yellow-orange legs are distinctive. When alarmed it raises its crest. Adult Little Blue Heron (22 in.) has a longer neck and is more slender and uniformly dark all over (see page 130).

CATTLE EGRET This exotic bird (17 in.), a native of Africa, recently colonized North America. It is still spreading into new areas. It usually feeds with cattle, but it nests in colonies with other herons. Young birds are all white. Other white herons are the Snowy Egret (20 in.) with its slender black bill and legs and yellow feet, the immature Little Blue Heron (22 in.) with greenish legs and feet and a pale base to the bill, and the Great Egret (32 in.) with yellow bill, black legs and feet (page 130).

TUNDRA (WHISTLING) SWAN   This very large (36 in.) all-white bird migrates from its arctic nesting grounds to its winter quarters in coastal United States. It feeds from the surface, using its long neck to reach aquatic vegetation. The introduced Mute Swan (40 in.) is spreading and has become common in city parks, on reservoirs and coastal bays in the Northeast and Midwest. Adults have an orange bill and gracefully curved neck. Often swims with wings arched over back.

CANADA GOOSE, a well-known and widely distributed bird, is recognized by its large size (16–25 in.), long black neck, and white cheeks. Geese swim with their necks straight up and fly in V-formation with their necks extended. They feed in ponds and estuaries, but also graze on grass and sprouting grain. In some places they have become so numerous they are considered pests. The smaller, dark, arctic-nesting Brant (17 in.), which winters in flocks on coastal bays, has a small white neck stripe instead of white cheeks.

MALLARD This large (16 in.), common duck of ponds and sloughs has two white bars bordering its blue wing patch that identify both the colorful male and the mottled brown female. The green head and white neck ring are also good field marks of the male. Mallards, like

other surface-feeding ducks, take off in a vertical leap. They feed by tipping in shallow water. Mallards have been domesticated and often produce hybrids with other duck species.

AMERICAN BLACK DUCK, a common marshland duck (16 in.), resembles the female Mallard, but is darker with whiter wing linings. Males have bright red legs and yellowish bills. Black Ducks prefer freshwater and tidal marshes and lakes in nesting season, brackish water in winter. The similar Mottled Duck (15 in.) is restricted to Florida and the Gulf Coast. The widespread Gadwall (14½ in.) has a white belly and a small rectangular white patch on the black trailing edge of the wing.

WOOD DUCK (13½ in.) is told in flight by its long tail, short neck, and the white trailing edge on its wing. Note the large white eye ring of the female and young. Usually found in wooded swamps or ponds, Wood Ducks fly low, dodging around trees; often nest in woodpecker cavities or nest boxes. A flying American Wigeon (14 in.) shows a large white patch on the forward edge of its wing. The male has a white crown and a broad green band through the eye.

NORTHERN PINTAIL   Spot the slim pintail (18½ in.) by the male's slender white neck and long, pointed tail. In all plumages flying birds show a white stripe on the trailing edge of the wing, which is the best field mark of the female. This common surface-feeding duck prefers fresh water. The tiny Green-winged Teal (10½ in.) has a broad green stripe across the face, contrasting with the plain brown head, and it has white borders before and behind the green wing patch.

CANVASBACK Note the white back and sides, sloping forehead, and long bill of this diving duck (15 in.). In flight note its large size. Female has pale brown head and neck. Locally common, but overall numbers have declined. Smaller Redhead (14½ in.) has gray body, more rounded forehead. Male Lesser Scaup (12 in.) has white

stripe down extended wing and may have glossy purple or purple-green head. Male Greater Scaup (14 in.) has a rounded black head with green sheen.

COMMON MERGANSER Mergansers are loonlike diving ducks with long, thin "toothed" bills used to catch fish. They fly low and white wing patches are visible in flight. The Common Merganser (18 in.) is strikingly white beneath. Note the sharp contrast between the female's chestnut-colored head and white throat. The Red-breasted Merganser (16 in.) has a reddish breast and a larger crest, and is strictly coastal in winter. The smaller Hooded Merganser (13 in.) has a fan-shaped white crest and is often seen in wooded swamps and lakes.

AMERICAN COOT (12 in.) nests in marsh vegetation, but often winters in open water. It is the only ducklike bird with a chalky white bill. When disturbed it either dives or skits over the water with feet and wings. The

closely related Common Moorhen (or Common Gallinule, 10½ in.) has a red bill and forehead and a white stripe under the wing. Both pump their neck while swimming.

KILLDEER (8 in.), a large upland plover, is told by its double breast band and (in flight) by its orange-brown rump and tail. It frequents open meadows and plowed fields, where its loud "killdeer" call resounds. It bobs its head as it walks. The downy young, which have only one breast band, leave the nest almost as soon as they hatch. The Semi-palmated Plover (5¾ in.) is much smaller, has only one breast band, and lacks the bright rump. It prefers mudflats and beaches.

COMMON SNIPE This shy bird (9 in.) of wet meadows and freshwater wetlands rises high in the spring air
at dusk and circles with an unforgettable "winnowing"
sound; otherwise it stays close to vegetation. Field marks
are very long bill, rather short legs, pointed wings, and
fast zigzag flight. The plump American Woodcock (8¼

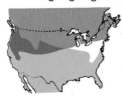

in.) of moist woods and fields has
rounded wings and a rich brown
color. Dowitchers (10 in.), of mudflats and beaches, have a conspicuous white rump, and in spring are
reddish-brown beneath.

LESSER YELLOWLEGS This gray and white sand-piper (8³⁄₄ in.) with its long, bright yellow legs is one of our common shorebirds. In flight note its white rump and tail, and slender, dark bill. The larger Greater Yellowlegs (11 in.) is very similar but has a longer, slightly upturned bill. Willets (13¹⁄₂ in.) are still larger and plumper, with dark legs and with bold black-and-white wing markings in flight. Still larger is the Whimbrel (14 in.) with its long down-curved bill and the Marbled Godwit (16 in.) with its up-curved bill.

SPOTTED SANDPIPER (6¼ in.) This is our only sandpiper with a strongly spotted breast. In many inland localities this is the most common shorebird and the only breeding sandpiper. The spots are present only in the breeding season, but the teetering walk and the shallow wing beats and low flight are distinctive. The Solitary Sandpiper (7 in.), seen during migration, has a white eye ring, and barred white feathers on the sides of the tail.

LEAST SANDPIPER Best known and the smallest of the small sandpipers (called "peeps"), this bird prefers mudflats and salt marshes. Note its small size (4¾ in.), rich brown back, streaking on the breast, yellowish legs, and short, slender bill. The Semipalmated (5 in.) and Western (5¼ in.) Sandpipers, often found with the Least, have grayer backs, stouter bills, and black legs; the Western has a longer, heavier bill and tends to feed in deeper water. The larger White-rumped Sandpiper (6¼ in.) has a distinct white rump.

HERRING GULL (20 in.) is abundant along the Atlantic Coast and parts of the interior. It is a great scavenger. Black wing tips of adults contrast with gray wings and back. Legs are flesh-colored. Immature birds are dull gray-brown, becoming whiter with maturity. California and Ring-billed Gulls (17 in.) are smaller with dull yellowish or greenish legs; Ring-billed has a black ring on the bill. Laughing Gull (13 in.) on the East Coast and Franklin's Gull (11 in.) in the West have darker backs and black heads.

COMMON TERN Terns are smaller, slimmer, and more graceful than gulls; wings are slender and tails often deeply forked. They dive headlong into sea or lakes after fish. Common Tern (14 in.) has a black-tipped, reddish bill, dusky wing tips, and deeply forked white tail. Forster's Tern (14 in.) is very similar but with orange bill and paler wing tips. The tiny Least Tern (8½ in.) has a yellow bill. Its flight is rapid and buoyant. The gull-sized Caspian Tern (20 in.) has a heavy blood-red bill and slightly forked tail.

TURKEY and BLACK VULTURES   are valuable scavengers that soar high in the sky. The more widespread Turkey Vulture (25 in.) soars with its wings raised slightly above horizontal. Adults have a naked red head and silver-gray feathers on the underside of their wings. The smaller Black Vulture (at right, 22 in.) of the Southwest

soars on horizontal wings and flaps more often than a Turkey Vulture. It has a dark head, as do young Turkey Vultures, and white patches on the underside of its wing tips. Its range is spreading northward.

OSPREY   The Osprey or Fish Hawk (22 in.) is common along coasts, but uncommon inland. It is smaller than an eagle, and no other large hawk has as much white below. It has large dark patches on its cheek and at the "wrist" of its wing. Ospreys soar over water with a characteristic backward bend of their wings. They often hover and plunge feet foremost after fish. Huge nest may be placed on an isolated tree, a channel marker, or a duck blind. Young Ospreys are similar to adults.

BALD EAGLE Eagles are large hawks that soar on horizontal wings. The white head and tail mark an adult Bald Eagle (32 in.), the U.S. national emblem. Younger birds are mostly dark brown with pale splotches under their wings and tail; it takes them several years to acquire

adult plumage. Bald Eagles are usually found near water, as fish is their favorite food. The Golden Eagle (32 in.) is all dark, except for immature birds which have a flash of white under the tail and wings.

COOPER'S HAWK (15½ in.) is typically a woodland bird, rarely soaring in the open except when migrating. Its short, rounded wings and long, rounded tail identify it in flight. The little Sharp-shinned Hawk (10½ in.) looks similar, but has a square-tipped tail and smaller head. The large Northern Goshawk (19 in.) has a light gray breast, dark gray back, and white line over the eye. Females of all are much larger than males; breasts of young are streaked lengthwise.

RED-TAILED HAWK is a large (18 in.) soaring hawk with broad wings and a fan-shaped tail that is chestnut above. Underparts are light except for a band of dark streaks across the belly. Young have a finely barred tail. Red-shouldered Hawk (16 in.), found in wooded stream valleys, is rusty below with narrow bands on tail. Other

soaring hawks include the crow-sized Broad-winged Hawk (13 in.) of northeastern woods with broad bands on its tail, and Swainson's Hawk (18 in.) of the West, with its broad, dark chest band.

AMERICAN KESTREL is the smallest (8½ in.) U.S. falcon—a hawk with long, pointed wings. It hovers in the air and drops on prey; often perches on telephone wires. Note rich reddish-brown back, tail, and crown. The slightly larger Merlin (12 in.) is uniformly dark above, heavily streaked below, and has broad black tail bars. The endangered Peregrine Falcon (15 in.) has heavy black mustache marks and a blue or brown back. It formerly nested on remote cliffs but has been reintroduced in many places and now nests on city buildings and bridges.

RING-NECKED PHEASANT This unmistakable Asian bird (27 in.) has been successfully introduced over much of the United States. It is a favorite game bird of farmlands, where it feeds on waste grain, occasionally causing local crop damage. The handsome male is unrivaled in its splendid coloring. The female is smaller, buffy brown all over. It is distinguished from the Sharp-tailed Grouse (see next page) by its larger size and longer tail. Pheasants and their relatives on the next two pages do not migrate.

RUFFED GROUSE (14 in.), an attractive chicken-like bird found in wooded areas, is usually not seen until it springs into the air with a loud whirring of wings. During spring courtship, males attract females by beating their wings to make a drumming sound. The fan-shaped tail with its broad, dark terminal band is the best field mark.

Prairie-Chickens (14 in.) of the midwest are finely barred with brown and white and have horizontal bars on the breast. The breast of the similar Sharp-tailed Grouse (15 in.) is streaked.

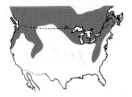

NORTHERN BOBWHITE (8 in.) is a small quail named after its call. Its small size, rich brown color, and stubby appearance make it hard to see in tall grass, but their call is easily recognized. Several other quails live in the West, including the Gambel's, California, and Mountain Quails (all 8–9 in.). They are plain olive or gray on the back and have head plumes. The grayish Scaled Quail (8 in.) of New Mexico has a white-tipped crest. Females of all species are duller colored than males.

Bobwhite

Bobwhite

Gambel's

ROCK DOVE (DOMESTIC PIGEON) is descended from the wild Rock Dove of European coastal cliffs. This chubby bird (11 in.) has a broad, fanned tail. Colors vary from slate-blue to brown to white. Their nesting habits make them unpopular tenants in cities. The large western Band-tailed Pigeon (13½ in.) has yellow legs and a pale tail band. The White-crowned Pigeon (11 in.) of the Florida Keys is all dark with a white crown. The tiny Common Ground-Dove of the far South is brownish, with flashy chestnut feathers on its wings.

MOURNING DOVE Browner and slimmer than the Rock Dove and with a long, pointed tail, the Mourning Dove (10½ in.) nests in every state and province. It is named for its melancholy call: "Coo-ah, coo, coo, coo." The white tail border is conspicuous in flight. Flight is rapid, and this dove is prized as a favorite game

species in many states. The White-winged Dove (10 in.) of the Southwest is similar, but a large white wing patch is conspicuous in flight. The southwestern Inca Dove (6½ in.) is like a miniature Mourning Dove.

YELLOW-BILLED CUCKOO Cuckoos are slender birds with long bills that are commonly found in open woods, orchards, and along wooded streams. The lower part of the bill of the Yellow-billed Cuckoo (11 in.) is yellow, and it has bright chestnut wing patches and large white tail spots. The less common Black-billed Cuckoo (11 in.) is found more to the north. Its bill is black, and it has plain brown wings and indistinct gray spots on its tail. Cuckoos are among the few birds that will eat hairy caterpillars.

BARN OWL (14 in.) is sometimes described as "monkey-faced" because it is the only North American owl with a white, heart-shaped face and dark eyes. Its light buff plumage is conspicuous, but rarely seen during the day because it roosts and nests in barns, church belfries, and hollow trees. The Barn Owl gives a hissing call at night and that has led to superstitions about its nature. However, Barn Owls are very helpful in controlling rodents injurious to orchards and garden crops.

GREAT HORNED OWL (20 in.), our largest owl, is aggressive and powerful. It nests on the ground, or in trees or caves. Like other owls, it is more likely to be heard than seen. Its call is a series of 5 to 7 deep hoots, all on the same pitch. The Barred Owl (17 in.) of the East and Northwest and Spotted Owl (16 in.) of the West have dark eyes, no ear tufts. The Barred Owl typically gives 8 hoots, the Spotted Owl 3 or 4.

EASTERN and WESTERN SCREECH-OWLS Recently separated into two species, these closely related nocturnal birds are told from other common owls by their small size (8 in.) and presence of ear tufts. Plumage of these two is almost identical, but gray and brown color phases occur. Both species whistle rather than screech. Keen eyesight and noiseless flight enable them to prey on field rodents. The terrestrial Burrowing Owl (8 in.) of the prairies and the Northern Saw-whet Owl (7 in.) of the North woods lack ear tufts.

Western   Eastern

CHIMNEY SWIFT Swifts are almost always in the air, flying with a batlike flight. Distinctive, streamlined birds, they usually fly in groups and migrate in large flocks. The short spiny tails of Chimney Swifts (5 in.) prop them against inside walls of chimneys when resting. Of the three western swifts, Vaux's Swift (4½ in.), found in forests, looks most like the Chimney. White-throated Swift (6½ in.), of steep canyons, and the rare Black Swift (7 in.) are colored as their names imply.

WHIP-POOR-WILL When resting on dead leaves, the nocturnal Whip-poor-will (9 in.) is almost invisible—more often heard than seen. It rarely flies by day. A rounded tail, buffy-tipped in the female, and absence of white in the wing distinguish it from the nighthawks.

The southeastern Chuck-will's-widow (11 in.) has buff on the throat and under the tail. The small western Common Poor-will (7 in.) has only tiny square white patches at the corners of the tail.

COMMON NIGHTHAWK (9 in.), a close relative of the Whip-poor-will, has slender, pointed wings and a long tail with slightly notched tip. In flight note its distinguishing white wing patch. Nighthawks are constantly in the air at night, flying in a zigzag path, circling, diving, and banking as they catch flying insects. The lower-flying Lesser Nighthawk (8 in.) of the Southwest has the white band nearer the tip of a more rounded wing. Young are similar to adults.

RUBY-THROATED HUMMINGBIRD   These eastern hummingbirds (3 in.) are gems of beauty and marvels in flight. They hover motionless and even fly backwards. They sip nectar from flowers and will come to brightly colored feeders filled with sugar water. Females and young are white-throated. Western hummingbirds include the similar

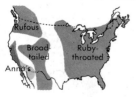

Broad-tailed (3¾ in.) of the southern Rockies; Anna's (3½ in.) of the Pacific Coast, with metallic red crown and throat; Black-chinned (3 in.) in the western mountains; and the Northwest's brown-backed Rufous (3½ in.).

BELTED KINGFISHER (12 in.) Where there are fish there are kingfishers, beating the air with irregular flaps and diving head first into the water. They also perch above water, watching for fish. Note their ragged crest and long, spearlike beak, and listen for their harsh rattling call. Illustration is of a female; the male lacks the chestnut on sides and breast. The tiny Green Kingfisher (7½ in.) of southern Texas has a dark green back and almost no crest.

RED-HEADED WOODPECKER (7½ in.) is the only eastern woodpecker with an entirely red head and neck. Its solid black back contrasts with its white underside and large white wing patches. Young have brown heads. Male Red-bellied Woodpeckers (8½ in.) of the East have a red crown and back of neck, a pale red patch on their belly, and black-and-white barring on their back. The western Acorn Woodpecker (8 in.) has a black chin, white cheeks and forehead, and red cap.

NORTHERN FLICKER (10½ in.), large and brown, is identified during its undulating flight by its white rump, black breast band, and flashes of bright yellow or red under its wings and tail. Like all woodpeckers, it nests in a tree cavity, but often goes to the ground to eat ants. The "Yellow-shafted Flicker" (above) is seen in the east and north, the "Red-shafted Flicker" in the west. The similar but less common species, Gilded Flicker, is found in the Southwest.

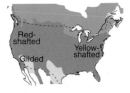

YELLOW-BELLIED SAPSUCKER (7½ in.) Sapsuckers dig rows of small holes that leave scars on trunks and branches of trees. They feed on the sap that oozes out and on the insects the sap attracts. Note the vertical white patch on the black wing. The Red-breasted Sapsucker (7¼ in.), found in the mountains of the Pacific coast, is similar but with head and breast solid red. The Red-naped Sapsucker (7½ in.) of the Rocky Mountains has a red patch on the back of its head.

DOWNY WOODPECKER   The Downy (5¾ in.) and Hairy (7½ in.) Woodpeckers are common and widespread and have similar plumage. The white stripe down the back is a good field mark for both. Only the males have the red spot on the back of the head. The Hairy Woodpecker is much larger than the Downy, has a heavier bill, and its outer tail feathers are entirely white. The Downy often feeds with chickadees, titmice, and nuthatches, and visits feeders in winter for suet and seeds.

EASTERN KINGBIRD (6³/₄ in.) darts from a perch on a branch or fence to catch insects in the air, then returns to its perch. The white tip on the tail marks this eastern species of flycatcher. The Gray Kingbird (7¹/₂ in.) of the Florida coast has an oversized bill and a gray notched tail. The Western Kingbird (7 in.)

has a gray head, yellow belly, and white outer tail feathers. The similar Cassin's Kingbird (7 in.) has only a narrow grayish tip on its tail. Young are similar to adults.

GREAT CRESTED FLYCATCHER is the only large (7 in.) eastern flycatcher with a rusty tail. The yellow belly and pale wing bars are good field marks. It is an orchard and forest bird. It typically uses shed snake skins in its nest, which is placed in a tree cavity or nest box. This flycatcher is told from the Western Kingbird by its tail color. The smaller, paler Ash-throated Flycatcher (6½ in.) replaces the Great Crested Flycatcher in the West. Young are like adults.

EASTERN PHOEBE (5³/₄ in.) If the persistent "fee-be" call doesn't identify this bird, its equally persistent tail-bobbing will. It is an active flycatcher, with no wing bars or eye ring. It nests in the shelter of a porch, eaves, or bridge. Say's Phoebe (6¹/₄ in.) is a western bird with rusty

breast and belly. Eastern and Western Wood Pewees (5¹/₄ in.) look like small Eastern Phoebes but have two distinct wing bars and do not bob their tails. They are common in woodlands.

LEAST FLYCATCHER is part of a genus of flycatchers called *Empidonax*. All share the eye ring and two whitish wing bars and are notoriously difficult to tell apart. They are best distinguished by habitat and voice. The Least, found in woods and parks, is smallest (4½ in.). The Acadian Flycatcher nests in southeastern forests and swamps, and the Willow in marshes and brushy pastures. In the West the Pacific Slope and Cordilleran Flycatchers have yellow bellies; but the drabber Hammond's, Gray, and Dusky are often simply identified as "empids."

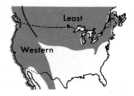

HORNED LARK Flocks of Horned Larks (6½ in.) walk across bare fields or along shores as they feed. Note the black breast band, yellow throat, black tail, and, at close range, the "horns." Young birds are streaked. This and the Sky Lark are true larks. Meadowlarks (page 117) belong to the blackbird subfamily. Although they are unre-

lated, the American Pipit (5½ in.) is sometimes mistaken for the Horned Lark. The American Pipit also walks, but has a lightly spotted buffy breast and long bobbing tail with white outer feathers.

PURPLE MARTIN   Martins are the largest (7 in.) and most conspicuous of the swallows, streamlined birds that do all of their feeding on the wing. In flight their wings are more triangular than other swallows'. Martins nest in colonies, most often in multicelled martin boxes. The uniform dark color of the male identifies it. Females and young have grayish breast and white belly. The Northern Rough-winged Swallow (4³/₄ in.), which nests singly in drain pipes or holes in gravel banks, is much smaller, with a plain brown back and chest.

TREE SWALLOW Unbroken blue-black above and white below makes the Tree Swallow (5 in.) easy to pick out from a mixed flock of migrating swallows. Female is duller. Young birds are brown-backed. In cold weather this swallow can substitute bayberries for insects, so it

can winter farther north than other swallows. The western Violet-green Swallow (4¾ in.) is similar with a large white patch on each side of its rump. Swallows are usually found near water.

BARN SWALLOW (6 in.) This is the one swallow with a long, deeply forked "swallow tail." Note the chestnut forehead and throat, and buff underparts. Young are duller with shorter tails. Nests in buildings and under bridges. The Cliff Swallow (5 in.) is similar, but with short, square tail, orange-brown rump, and buff forehead. The Bank Swallow (4¾ in.), which nests in large colonies in burrows in stream banks and gravel pits, has a brown back and a brownish-gray band across its white breast.

BLACK-BILLED MAGPIE No other birds resemble the large black-and-white magpies with their sweeping tails. The two species, Black-billed (18 in.) and Yellow-billed (16 in.) Magpies, are distinguished by bill color and geography. The Yellow-billed Magpie lives only in the central California valleys. Magpies fly and feed in

flocks. Their mixed diet includes fruits, melons, and other crop plants. They often live around ranches, and occasionally these relatives of the crows become serious local pests.

AMERICAN CROW   People often confuse two related birds with the familiar all-black American Crow (17 in.). The coastal Fish Crow (15 in.) is similar, but has a longer tail, smaller head and bill, and short nasal call: "cuh cuh." The large Common Raven (21 in.), rare in much of the East, has a heavy beak, rough throat feathers, and a croaking call. It soars in flight, showing the wedge-shaped tail.

BLUE JAY   No other bird is like the noisy blue, black, and white Blue Jay (10 in.). Of the western jays, Steller's (11 in.) has a black head, throat, and breast, and long black crest (page 18). The short-tailed, crestless Pinyon Jay (9 in.) is dull blue with a darker crown. The Western

Scrub-Jay (10 in.) is widespread west of the Rockies. Its close relative, the Florida Scrub-Jay (10 in.), is found in central Florida. Both have blue caps, wings, and tails, and whitish underparts.

WHITE-BREASTED NUTHATCH Nuthatches creep down tree trunks head first, and often visit feeders. The White-breasted Nuthatch (5 in.), with its white breast, throat, and face, is common in deciduous woods. Other nuthatches prefer conifers. The smaller Red-breasted Nuthatch (4 in.) has orange-brown underparts and a dark line through the eye. The Brown-headed Nuthatch (4 in.) of the southeast pine woods has a chocolate cap; the tiny western Pygmy Nuthatch (3½ in.) a brownish-gray cap. Both caps come down to the eye.

BLACK-CAPPED CHICKADEE (4½ in.) is a frequent visitor to feeders and often feeds upside down. Its *chick-a-dee-dee-dee* call gives it its name. The smaller Carolina Chickadee (4¼ in.) of the Southeast looks very similar but has less buff on the sides and less white on the wings. The

brown-capped Boreal Chickadee (4¼ in.) is a winter visitor along the Canadian border. The western Chestnut-backed Chickadee (4¼ in.) has a dull brown cap and a bright chestnut back and rump.

TUFTED TITMOUSE The pointed crest and persistent whistled "peter, peter" call distinguish the Tufted Titmouse (5½ in.). It is told from chickadees by the lack of the black bib, and from the Nuthatches by the stubby bill and perching habit. The Oak and Juniper Titmice of the West (5 in.) lack the rusty flanks. The slender, long-tailed Bushtit (3½ in.) of the arid West is plain gray-brown above, with no crest; crown is brown or gray. Young are similar to adults.

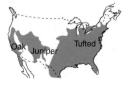

BROWN CREEPER This is the only small (4³/₄ in.) brown tree-creeping bird. Its underparts are white, its tail stiff. It works its way up the tree in a spiral, searching for insects and insect eggs it digs out with its curved bill. Then it flies to the base of a nearby tree and climbs up again. As their calls are high-pitched and their colors blend well with bark, these birds may be hard to detect. They prefer

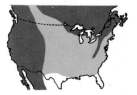

open mature woods, nesting under loose bark. They feed in the company of chickadees, kinglets, and woodpeckers. In winter they eat suet in feeders placed on tree trunks. Young are like adults.

HOUSE WREN   Wrens are small, chunky brown birds that usually carry their tail upright. The House Wren (4¼ in.) is a garden bird that lacks distinct markings. The tiny northern Winter Wren (3¼ in.) has a dark belly. Carolina Wren (4¾ in.) of the Southeast has a broad white eye stripe, ruddy back, and buff underparts. Western wrens include Bewick's Wren (4½ in.) with a white eye stripe and long tail with narrow white border, Canyon Wren (4½ in.) with white breast and dark belly, Rock Wren (4¾ in.) with faint breast streaks and buff-fringed tail, and the huge Cactus Wren (6½ in.) of the deserts.

RUBY-CROWNED KINGLET Kinglets are among our smallest birds (3³⁄₄ in.) and are primarily winter visitors. Their small, chunky bodies, stubby tails, and dull olive color are distinctive. Kinglets frequently flick their wings. The red crown of the Ruby-crowned Kinglet is often hidden, but the large eye ring will distinguish this species when its ruby crown does not

show. Female lacks ruby crown. Kinglets breed in northern spruce-fir forest. In winter they are common in thickets and woodlands and are often seen in shrubbery around buildings.

GOLDEN-CROWNED KINGLET (3½ in.) is the more showy of our two American species. The female has a golden crown bordered with black and white. The male has an additional orange stripe through the center of the golden crown. These kinglets are often seen feeding on the branches of firs, spruce, and other conifers, but in winter they also use deciduous woods. They eat insects, so are not attracted to feeding stations, although they are often found with chickadees, nuthatches, creepers, and woodpeckers in winter. Common call is three to five very high notes on the same pitch.

BLUE-GRAY GNATCATCHER (4 in.) is common in the South. Active birds, they are difficult to see because they live in treetops, feeding on insects. The blue-gray back, whitish underparts, and white eye ring are helpful field marks, as is their habit of jerking their tail. Native to moist woods and thickets of the South, their range is expanding northward.

The male Black-tailed Gnatcatcher (3³/₄ in.) of southwestern deserts and male California Gnatcatcher (4 in.) of southwest California scrublands have black caps. The tails of both species are black beneath.

EASTERN BLUEBIRD (5½ in.) is an early spring migrant in the North. It is a member of the thrush family. No other blue bird has a chestnut-brown breast. The Western Bluebird (5½ in.) has chestnut on the back as well. The adult male Mountain Bluebird (6 in.) of the Rockies has a lighter sky-blue back, pale blue breast, and white belly. Female bluebirds are much duller colored. Bluebirds were declining in many areas, but an extensive program of furnishing specially designed nesting boxes has led to a recovery.

Western

Eastern

WOOD THRUSH The spotted thrushes are typically woodland birds. Wood Thrushes (7 in.) are common in deciduous woods. They are recognized by their chestnut-brown backs, brighter heads, heavily spotted breasts, and clear, flutelike songs. The Veery (6 in.), which requires moist woods, also has a bright unmarked red-brown back, but with head and tail the same color as the back; it has only faint spotting on its breast. The long-tailed Brown Thrasher (page 91) has a streaked breast, but its eye is yellow.

HERMIT THRUSH (7 in.) reverses the Wood Thrush's color pattern: its tail is much brighter than its back. Its loud, liquid song is heard in the mountains of the North Woods. Other thrushes also have dull, olive-brown backs. Swainson's Thrush (6¼ in.) has a buff eye ring and buff cheeks. The migrant Gray-cheeked Thrush (6¼ in.), which nests in the far North, and the similar Bicknell's Thrush (6¼ in.), of northeastern mountaintops, have gray cheeks with no eye ring.

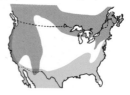

AMERICAN ROBIN   One of the most common native birds of towns and suburbs, the robin (8½ in.) nests in every state except Hawaii and in every Canadian province. It is the largest thrush, and young robins have heavily spotted breasts characteristic of thrushes. Females are similar to adult males, but duller colored. Colonialists

named the robin after a small European thrush with a much redder breast. The Varied Thrush (8 in.) of the Pacific states is similar to the robin but has a black breast band (page 130).

GRAY CATBIRD (7³/₄ in.) gets its name from its mewing call. It feeds and nests low in shrubs and vines, often near houses or moist thickets, and will sometimes hide in low shrubs and make a variety of songs and sounds. Catbirds are slate-gray except for a black cap and a chestnut patch under the base of the tail. The slender bill and long, rounded tail distinguish it from other dark birds its size. Young are similar to adults.

NORTHERN MOCKINGBIRD "Listen to the mockingbird..." goes the song, and the mockingbird (9 in.) is, indeed, worth hearing. Its song imitates other birds' songs perfectly, with original phrases added. Mockingbirds nest around homes, perch on chimneys and television antennas. White patches on wings and tail are conspicuous in flight. The Loggerhead Shrike (7 in., page 93), which also perches on wires and fences, is chunkier, with a thick bill and black mask.

BROWN THRASHER Related to the mockingbirds, thrashers have the same long rounded tails; most have down-curved bills. They feed and nest near the ground. The widespread Brown Thrasher (10 in.) is the richest chestnut above and streaked with brown below. The only western thrasher with heavy streaks, Sage Thrasher (7 in.), has white tips on its outer tail feathers. Le Conte's Thrasher (9¼ in.) is an ashy-gray desert bird with a plain breast. The California Thrasher (10 in.) is dark brown and unstreaked with a long down-curved bill; no wing bars.

CEDAR WAXWING (5¾ in.) These warm-brown, crested birds cannot be mistaken, especially when a whole flock is feeding on berries. Watch for the wide yellow tail band. Young are faintly streaked below and have a smaller crest. The grayer Bohemian Waxwing (6¼ in.) of the Northwest has bright cinnamon instead of white under the base of its tail. Waxwings get their name from the waxy red tips on some of an adult's wing feathers.

LOGGERHEAD SHRIKE (7 in.) Shrikes swoop down on their prey from a perch. Their rapid wing beats and bounding flight are distinctive. They hunt insects, rodents, and small birds, and often hang uneaten prey on thorns or barbed-wire fences. Shrikes resemble mocking-birds, but are chunkier and have a black eye mask and heavy hooked bill. The Northern Shrike (8 in.) is seen only in winter in the northern states. Its breast is faintly barred. The decline in the shrike population is a cause for concern.

EUROPEAN STARLING (6 in.) Introduced into New York in 1890, starlings have been spreading ever since. In some places they are a nuisance and even a pest. But they are handsome birds, given to musical song and mimicry. Sunlight on their plumage makes a rainbow of colors.

Note the short tail, plump body, and (in spring and summer) the yellow bill. Young birds are uniform brown with dark bills, and adults in winter are speckled with white.

Yellow Warbler

WARBLERS

Warblers are small, active woodland birds with slender, straight bills used for catching crawling or flying insects. Warblers are found only in the New World. There are about 110 species in the Warbler family, about half of which are regularly found in North America. To many, warblers are the most exciting birds to watch because of their many species, bright colors, distinctive songs, and migratory habits.

Most warblers winter in the tropics and migrate north to their breeding grounds in April and May. Males migrate a few days ahead of the duller-colored females. The best time to see them is before the trees are in full leaf. As many as 25 or 20 species may be found on some locations on a warm May morning.

When they return south for the winter, many warblers have molted to a duller color and are less easy to identify. By November most warblers have left for their winter homes in the tropics, but the Yellow-rumped Warbler (page 100) can be found all winter in some southern and coastal locations.

The song of most warblers is not really a warble. Many males have one song for warning other males to stay away, and another to attract females. Most of these songs are thin and unmusical. North American warblers often can be seen high in trees, singing or searching for insects.

YELLOW WARBLER (4 in.) is a plump, yellow warbler with a short tail. The male has distinctive chestnut streaks on his breast and a bright song. It prefers

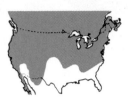

shrubs and low trees near streams, lakes, marshes, and swamps. The Orange-crowned Warbler (4½ in.) is duller yellow-green all over, with no wing bars or tail spots, and a small orange crown that is seldom seen.

BLACK-AND-WHITE WARBLER Only two eastern warblers are striped black and white: the common Black-and-white Warbler (4½ in.) and the Blackpoll Warbler (4½ in.), which has a solid black crown and is seen only

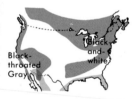

during migration. The Black-and-white moves up and down trunks and large branches like a nuthatch. Female and young lack the black throat. The western Black-throated Gray Warbler has a plain, almost unstreaked back.

Black-and-white

Black-throated Gray

BLACK-THROATED BLUE WARBLER This warbler (4½ in.) is really well named. No other north American bird has a blue back and black throat. The only distin-

guishing mark on the plain olive female is the small white wing spot. The Black-throated Green Warbler (4½ in.) of the East has a yellow-green back and golden face. The Cerulean Warbler (4 in.) of the Midwest is blue above with a narrow black necklace.

COMMON YELLOWTHROAT (4¼ in.) is a common warbler of marshes and moist grassy fields. A black mask and yellow throat mark the male. The female has a yellow throat and a whitish eye ring, but no mask. Neither has wing bars. The Kentucky Warbler (4½ in.) has bold yellow "spectacles," black crown and sideburns, and entirely yellow underparts. It is found in dense woodlands of the southeast.

OVENBIRD (5 in.) is a ground-loving woodland warbler often seen walking, instead of hopping, in the leaves with its tail bobbing. It resembles a small thrush: plain olive brown above with bold streaks on its breast. The orange crown with black borders and a narrow eye ring make identification positive. Its "teacher, teacher, teacher" song is easy to remember. Watch for it in eastern deciduous forests. Young lack the orange crown.

NORTHERN WATERTHRUSH These plump warblers stay on the ground near wooded swamps and brooks. The Northern Waterthrush (5 in.) has a distinct yellowish cast to the heavily streaked underparts, and usually a buffy eye line. The more southern Louisiana Waterthrush (5¼ in.) is whiter below, except for the buffy lower flanks; its throat is unstreaked, the eye line white and broader. Both species walk, rather than hop, bobbing their tails like sandpipers.

YELLOW-RUMPED WARBLER (4¾ in.) migrates earlier in spring and later in fall than other warblers. It has two subspecies: "Myrtle Warbler" and "Audubon's Warbler." Both have a yellow rump, crown, and side

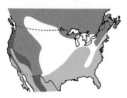

patches. "Audubon's" also has a yellow throat. Females, young, and winter birds are browner. The Magnolia Warbler (4¼ in.) of the East also has a yellow rump. It is told by its black-streaked yellow breast and bold white patches on the wings and tail.

AMERICAN REDSTART The orange and black male (4½ in.) is a striking bird of moist deciduous forests. The female is yellow and olive-gray, but with

the same pattern. Redstarts continually flit about and catch insects flycatcher fashion. The Painted Redstart (4½ in.) of evergreen forests in Arizona and New Mexico has a red breast, flashy white wing and tail patches.

WILSON'S WARBLER A small (4¼ in.), very active warbler, unbroken yellow below, plain olive-yellow above. There are no wing bars or tail spots. The female

lacks the black cap. It prefers moist thickets and swamps and is especially fond of willows. Hooded Warbler (4½ in.) of southeastern forests is similar except male has a black head and throat with yellow face; both sexes have white tail spots.

RED-EYED VIREO   Vireos are larger and less active than warblers. The Red-eyed (5 in.), common in deciduous forests, has a gray crown bordered with black, a broad white line above the red eye, and no wing bars. The dark-eyed Warbling Vireo (4¾ in.) lacks dark head marks. A pale yellow eye ring and two wing bars help

identify the White-eyed Vireo (4½ in.). The Yellow-throated Vireo (5 in.) of the East and the blue-headed Vireo (4¾ in.) have broad wing bars and eye rings. All young have brown eyes.

SCARLET TANAGER (6¼ in.) The male is our only red bird with black wings. The female is uniform yellow-green with dusky wings. The male Summer Tanager (6½ in.) of the South is entirely red, its mate orange-yellow. It prefers pine woods, while the Scarlet uses mixed or deciduous. The Western Tanager (6¼ in.) is bright yellow with black back and wings. It is the only tanager that has wing bars. Adult males have red heads. Tanagers can be told from orioles by their shorter, heavier bills.

NORTHERN CARDINAL The cardinal (7¾ in.) is the only eastern red bird with a crest. The heavy red bill, with black at the base, is a good field mark. The light brown female has the crest and red bill, but little red on the body. Young have dusky bills. Cardinals are common in shrubbery, hedgerows, and wood margins.

In recent years the cardinal has gradually spread northward. The crested Pyrrhuloxia (7½ in.) of the Southwest is mostly gray with red face, crest, breast, and tail, and the general cardinal shape.

ROSE-BREASTED GROSBEAK   The male (7¼ in.), nearly all black and white, flashes a deep rose patch on its breast. The female is streaked yellow-brown and white like an overgrown sparrow. Like all grosbeaks they have heavy conical bills. The closely related Black-headed Grosbeak (7¼ in.) of the west also has the black head and back, but its entire underparts are orange-brown. The Evening Grosbeak (7¼ in.) is a chunky, noisy finch of the North and western mountains. It has a dark brown head, bright yellow rump and belly, and black-and-white wings and tail.

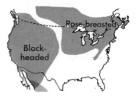

Rose-breasted

Black-headed

INDIGO BUNTING (4½ in.) is our only small bird that is entirely blue. Female is warm brown with very faint breast streaks. They live in hedgerows and wood margins. The southern Blue Grosbeak (6¼ in.) is much larger with chestnut wing bars and a much heavier bill. Other buntings are also splashes of brilliant color. The Lazuli Bunting (5½ in.) of the West is similar to the Indigo, but has white wing

bars, chestnut breast, and white belly. The male Painted Bunting (4½ in.) of the South is a showy combination of red below and blue and green above; but the female is pale yellow-green.

EASTERN TOWHEE (7¼ in.) may be told by its "chewink" call and by its black back and tail (with white tip), white belly, and chestnut side patches. Adult's eyes are bright red (white in southeastern birds). The female is brown instead of black. This species nests in thickets at the edges of both coniferous and deciduous woods. In the west, the similar Spotted Towhee (7¼ in.) has many small white spots on its wings and back. All towhees are ground-feeders that scratch vigorously in the dead leaves for insects and seeds.

CALIFORNIA TOWHEE and CANYON TOWHEE

These western towhees were formally considered one species. The California (7¾ in.) is plain brown above, gray below, with a slightly browner cap. It is found in chaparral and parks, and is currently threatened. The Canyon (7¼ in.) is pale gray rather than brown, with chestnut cap, and dark central breast spot. Favored habitats are hill country and desert canyons. Albert's Towhee (7¾ in.) of Southwest deserts is similar, but has a black face. Green-tailed Towhee (6¼ in.) of the western mountains has a green back, reddish crown, white throat, and gray sides.

Chipping Sparrow

SPARROWS

Worldwide there are nearly 300 species of sparrows, of which 52 have been recorded in North America north of Mexico. Towhees, juncos, and some less well-known birds such as grassquits and longspurs are included in these totals. The only ones discussed here are birds that occur over much of the continent and are likely to be found by beginners.

Sparrows are small to medium-sized birds with stout conical bills adapted for crushing seeds, which are their main diet. Seed-eaters have a better chance for winter survival in the North than do insect-eaters, so sparrows are conspicuous winter residents in areas where daytime winter temperatures are likely to remain below freezing for several consecutive days.

Most sparrows have streaked backs. Head and breast patterns can be used to identify most species. Each species has its own particular nesting habitat in summer, but during migration and in winter several species often flock together. Sparrows are short-distance migrants, wintering largely within the United States and southern Canada. They arrive on their breeding grounds early in spring. Most species prefer fields rather than woodlands.

FIELD SPARROW   This common sparrow (5 in.) of brushy fields displays a reddish-brown crown; its plain

breast, pink bill and legs, and broad gray eye ring clinch its identification. Its song is an accelerating series of slurred whistles. Compare the Field Sparrow with the American Tree, Chipping, and Swamp Sparrows, which have the same reddish cap.

AMERICAN TREE SPARROW   The bright reddish cap together with the single dark breast spot identifies the American Tree Sparrow (5¼ in.). Note also that the bill is dark above, yellowish below. The sweet song is rarely heard in its winter range. This bird is not related to the

Eurasian Tree Sparrow (5 in.), which has been introduced into southern Illinois and which looks like a House Sparrow with a small black cheek patch and brown crown.

VESPER SPARROW   (5½ in.) is a bird of large open fields marked by white outer tail feathers and small chestnut wing patches. The Vesper resembles the Savannah Sparrow (4¾ in.), but does not have a bold yellow or white eyebrow. The Song Sparrow (page 114) lack the Vesper's

wing patch. The Lark Sparrow (5¾ in.) of the West has a broad white fringe around the tail, large chestnut ear patch, central breast spot, and a very distinctive pattern of brown and white on the head.

CHIPPING SPARROW   This small sparrow (4½ in.) is told by its reddish crown, clear white underparts, white line over the eye, black line through the eye, and black bill. Young have streaked crowns with little or no red. The song is a rapid series of unmusical "chips" on

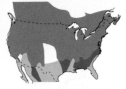

the same pitch. The Chipping Sparrow prefers lawns, golf courses, and other short-grass habitats.

WHITE-CROWNED SPARROW   The black-and-white crown, erect posture, plain gray breast and throat, and pink or yellowish bill identify this sparrow (5¾ in.). Young have brown and buff head stripes. Western birds use suburban habitats, but eastern birds prefer hedge-

rows bordered by large fields. The Golden-crowned Sparrow (6¼ in.), which winters in the Pacific states, differs by having a dull yellow crown bordered with black.

WHITE-THROATED SPARROW   This bird (5¾ in.) is told from the preceding by a distinct white throat and a small spot of yellow before the eye. It lacks the erect posture and gray hind neck of the White-crowned Sparrow. Its whistled "Old Sam Peabody Peabody Peabody"

song is familiar in the North woods in summer, and can also be heard on warm winter mornings. In winter it prefers wood margins and thickets, and is never found far from cover.

SONG SPARROW   A large brown center spot on a boldly streaked breast, and a rather long, rounded tail that it pumps as it flies, are the field marks of the Song Sparrow (5½ in.). Its melodious, varied song, one of the first signs of

spring, is easy to recognize. At all seasons Song Sparrows are found in hedgerows, shrubbery, and weedy fields. The Smaller Lincoln's Sparrow (4¾ in.), most common in the West, is similar but with a buff breast band crossed by fine dark streaks.

SWAMP SPARROW   (5 in.) Note the Swamp Sparrow's white throat, red-brown crown, plain gray breast,

and rounded tail. The rusty wings, dark bill, and the broad gray stripe over the eye (buffy in young birds) will confirm the identification. It prefers wet, brushy habitats in all seasons. Its song is a slow musical trill.

FOX SPARROW   (6¼ in.) is our largest true sparrow. Its markings are highly variable. Most subspecies have a bright red-brown tail and heavily streaked breast, but some are much darker, especially in the Pacific Northwest. Though a little like a Hermit Thrush

(page 87) in size and markings, the Fox Sparrow has a heavier bill and more conspicuous breast streaks. It frequents woods and thickets, and scratches in dry leaves with both feet at once like a towhee.

DARK-EYED JUNCO (5¼ in.) is usually seen near the ground, feeding on seeds. Its gray or brown back contrasts with its whitish belly and clear white outer tail feathers. The female is browner. Several different juncos are found in North America, but those with dark eyes are all considered one species. In different places they are

known as Oregon Juncos or Slate-colored Juncos, both of which are recognized names for distinctive subspecies. Juncos are common nesting birds in the North woods, preferring conifers. They are one of the most frequent visitors to feeders in winter.

EASTERN MEADOWLARK (8½ in.) prefers pastures, meadows, and grain fields. The very similar Western Meadowlark (8½ in.) is slightly paler on the back, and the yellow of the throat goes higher on the cheek. Note the black "V" on the yellow breast of the meadowlarks. Meadowlarks walk about on open ground. When they are startled, they fly away with a distinctive pattern that alternates rapid wingbeats and glides. The Western Meadowlark's song is louder and more flutelike than the simple whistle of the Eastern. Young of both species are like the adults.

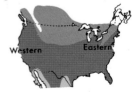

BOBOLINK The male (6 in.), the only North American songbird that is light above, all-black below, is easy to identify. However, the female and the male in fall are sparrowlike, with buff breasts and black-and-buff stripes on the crown. In summer it eats insects in hayfields, but

in fall it may damage rice crops. The other grains it eats are of no commercial value. The Bobolink winters in South America. Its song is one of the most beautiful of bird songs.

RED-WINGED BLACKBIRD   The male (7¼ in.) is unique with its red shoulders, margined with buff. The female is dusky brown above with a heavily streaked breast and generally with no hint of the red shoulder. The Tricolored Blackbird (7½ in.) of California's central valleys has deeper red shoulders with a white margin. Both species are abundant marsh and field birds, nesting in reeds, cattails, and shrubs. They form large flocks during fall, winter, and spring.

BREWER'S BLACKBIRD (8 in.) This is the blackbird of western ranches and corrals. The yellow eye of the male and the purplish tinge to its head feathers are field marks. It walks with its wings slightly drooping. The female is plain brownish gray with brown eyes. The Rusty

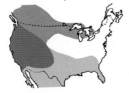

Blackbird (8 in.) of the East is similar, but with white eyes. It has rusty tips on its feathers in fall and winter, but is black the rest of the year. The Rusty Blackbird seldom flocks with other blackbirds.

COMMON GRACKLE Grackles are abundant, large blackbirds with long wedge-shaped tails. The Common Grackle (10-12 in.) is a familiar suburban and farmland bird that nests in colonies in evergreen trees. Note the iridescent plumage of the male. The Boat-tailed Grackle (12-16 in.) is found along the coast from Delaware to Texas, and the Great-tailed Grackle (12-16 in.) is becoming abundant in the southern Great Plains. Female grackles are much smaller than males.

BROWN-HEADED COWBIRD (6½ in.) has the unfortunate habit of always laying its eggs in-nests of other birds. Its eggs hatch sooner than those of its host; only the fast-growing cowbirds survive. The cowbird is our smallest blackbird, and the only one with a brown head.

It gets its name from its habit of feeding with cattle. Like other blackbirds, they walk, but they hold their tails higher when walking than do their relatives. The female is uniform mouse-gray.

BALTIMORE ORIOLE With its orange underside and black hood, the male (7 in.) is one of the showiest birds of the east. Females are brownish-orange above, dull orange-yellow below, with two pale wing bars. The Orchard Oriole (6 in.), also of the east, is similar, but brick-red. The female Orchard Oriole is greenish-yellow. In the west, male Bullock's Orioles (7 in.) have orange on the sides of their head and over the eye, and bold white patches on their wings. Young orioles look similar to females.

PURPLE FINCH   The male Purple Finch (5½ in.) is old-rose in color, not purple. Females are sparrowlike, streaked brown and white with a distinctive dark streak at the side of the throat. Both sexes have the heavy seed-crushing bill, pale line over the eye, and notched tail. Feeders with sunflower seeds attract flocks of Purple Finches in winter. In the West, the similar Cassin's Finch

(6 in.) is recognized by the contrast between its brilliant red crown and the browner hind neck and back. Both species nest in conifers but are often found in deciduous trees and shrubs in winter.

HOUSE FINCH This abundant suburban bird (5¼ in.) is easily attracted to feeders. A native of the Southwest, a flock was released on Long Island in the 1940's, and the descendants have spread rapidly across the continent. The male has more brown on its wings than the Purple Finch (facing page). The female is streaked grayish-brown, but lacks the female Purple Finch's prominent line over the eye and the dark streak beside the throat.

AMERICAN GOLDFINCH   The yellow body, black
cap and wings mark the American Goldfinch (4¼ in.).
In flight it is recognized by its roller-coaster flight and
its clear song. It is a bird of weedy fields and meadows,
feeding near the ground, and nesting in young trees.
Female, young, and winter males are dull yellow-brown,
with wing bars but no black on the head. The western

Lesser Goldfinch (3¾ in.) is similar,
with black crown, but dark (green
or black) back and duller yellow
breast. Sunflower or thistle seeds
will attract goldfinches to feeding
stations.

HOUSE SPARROW This bird (5¼ in.), misnamed English Sparrow, is a native of Europe belonging to the Old World Sparrow family. Imported from England in 1850, it became established, spread rapidly, and is now widespread. The gray crown and black throat of the male are characteristic, as are the unstreaked brown crown and broad buff line over the eye of the female. Unlike our native sparrows, the House Sparrow nests in cavities and bird boxes. It is an aggressive species, driving native birds from feeders and nest boxes.

MIGRATIONS OF BIRDS

Arctic Tern (13 in.): grayish; red bill; black cap.

Most swimming birds that depend on flying or crawling insects cannot winter in cold climates. Some seed-eaters also migrate. Some birds migrate by day, others by night. No one knows just how birds find their way from their summer to their winter homes.

Migrations north and south are best known. Some birds move only a few hundred miles from their breeding to their winter range; others cover several thousand. Scarlet Tanagers travel from Peru to northern U.S.

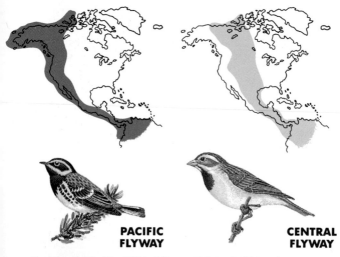

PACIFIC FLYWAY

Townsend's Warbler (4¼ in.) flies from Alaska and Yukon to Central America.

CENTRAL FLYWAY

Dickcissel (5¾ in.) migrates in enormous numbers from our grasslands to South America.

and back. Some warblers, vireos, and flycatchers travel even farther. The champion migrant is the Arctic Tern; some breed in the Arctic and winter in the Antarctic, 11,000 miles away. They fly over 25,000 miles a year and cross the Atlantic in their migration.

Four North American flyways form connecting paths between northern breeding grounds and wintering areas in the southern United States, Mexico, Cuba, and South America. Their use by waterfowl is best known, though most migrating birds use them. Flyways overlap in the breeding grounds, though each tends to have its own population.

The periods of spring and fall migrations are the times you will see the most birds. See pages 131-153 for when to look for migrants.

MISSISSIPPI FLYWAY

Upland Sandpiper (10 in.) migrates from the Arctic and the prairies to central South America.

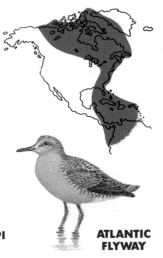

ATLANTIC FLYWAY

Red Knot (8½ in.) concentrates on the Atlantic coast enroute from the Arctic to Chile.

Varied Thrush (8 in.): Robin-like, black bar on orange breast.

Evening Grosbeak (7¼ in.): larger than goldfinch; huge beak.

Besides north and south migrations, vertical movements occur in high mountains. Summer residents nest high among spruce and fir in summer, later moving down to foothills and valleys for more dependable winter food.

Many species normally migrating farther north breed at high elevations in the mountains. Another pattern is

that shown by young herons and eagles. Soon after they leave the nest, they wander northward. By late summer or early fall many are hundreds of miles north of their nesting grounds. Before winter they go south again.

Left: **Great Egret** (32 in.), a large heron, all white; black legs, yellow bill. Right: **Little Blue Heron** (22 in.), smaller than Great Blue (page 23). Legs greenish. Young white; blue tint on wings.

THE BIRDS AT A GLANCE

The tables on pages 132-153 give concisely, for each bird illustrated, a wealth of facts on migration, nests and eggs, and feeding habits.

The information on migration is given by key cities: DC—Washington, D.C.; NY—New York; B—Boston; StL—St. Louis; SF—San Francisco; P—Portland, Oreg. You can estimate the arrival of birds in your region from dates for the nearest key city. There is about a week's difference between DC and NY and between NY and B for most migrating birds.

Birds found in an area the year round are listed as "permanent residents." For "summer residents" (SR), which come north in the spring, stay all summer, and depart in the fall, the table gives the average dates of arrival and departure. Average dates for "winter residents" (WR) are similarly given. Finally, some birds come north in the spring and, after staying a while, continue northward. These can be seen for only a few weeks in spring and fall. These birds are "transients" (Tr). Approximate dates for all birds are given in abbreviated form: E, M, and L stand for "early," "middle," and "late." "E-Apr" means early April and "M-Oct" stands for middle October.

Local weather, food supply, and other factors influence arrival and departure of birds. After several years, your own personal records may prove a better local guide than the abbreviated data given here, especially if you compare dates with those recorded by other observers in your county.

Birds and their nests and eggs are protected by federal and state laws. We do not encourage visiting nests, but if a nest is found, the information on pages 132-153 will help to identify the owner.

Page	Name	Migration		Eggs	
		Arrive	Depart	Size (in.)	No.
21	Common Loon	DC E-Oct B L-Sept StL E-Apr SF E-Oct	WR M-May WR L-May Tr L-Nov WR E-May	3.5 × 2.2 Variable; greenish or dull brown with faint black spots.	2
22	Pied-billed Grebe	DC M-Mar B E-Apr StL M-Mar P Permanent Resident	SR L-Oct SR M-Oct SR L-Nov	1.7 × 1.1 Very light blue-green, darker or buff; unmarked.	4-8
23	Great Blue Heron	NY E-Apr B E-Apr StL E-Mar SF Permanent Resident	SR L-Nov SR M-Nov SR L-Nov	2.4 × 1.8 Pale bluish green to dull blue; unmarked.	3-4
24	Green Heron	DC M-Apr B L-Apr StL M-Apr SF M-Mar	SR E-Oct SR M-Sept SR L-Sept SR L-Oct	1.5 × 1.1 Pale greenish or greenish blue; unmarked.	3-6
25	Cattle Egret	DC M-Apr NY L-Apr StL E-May	Tr M-Oct SR E-Oct SR L-Aug	1.8 × 1.3 Very pale green.	3-9
26	Tundra Swan	DC M-Nov StL M-Oct SF E-Oct	WR M-Apr WR L-Apr WR E-Apr	4.3 × 2.8 White or pale yellow.	2-6
27	Canada Goose	DC L-Sept B L-Sept StL E-Oct P M-Sept	WR M-Apr Tr L-Apr WR M-Apr WR M-May	3.4 × 2.3 Cream to dull greenish white. Later buffy and mottled.	4-10
28	Mallard	DC Permanent Resident NY E-Oct StL E-Sept P Permanent Resident	WR M-Apr WR E-May	2.3 × 1.6 Pale greenish to grayish buff.	6-12
29	American Black Duck	DC Permanent Resident NY Permanent Resident B Permanent Resident StL L-Oct	WR E-Apr	2.3 × 1.7 Grayish white to greenish buff. Similar to Mallard.	6-12
30	Wood Duck	DC L-Feb NY M-Mar StL M-Feb P Permanent Resident	SR M-Nov SR E-Nov SR L-Nov	2.0 × 1.6 Dull cream to buff.	8-15

Nests		Food
Materials	Location	
Vegetable debris.	On ground on small island or near shore of lake or pond.	Mainly fish; crabs, some insects and marine algae.
Decaying vegetation.	In shallow water. Floating among rushes in lakes and ponds.	Crayfish, crustaceans, small fish, and insects.
Sticks.	High up in tree or cliff near water.	Mainly fish; also crustaceans, frogs, and mice.
Sticks and twigs.	In trees, but near water; occasionally on ground.	Mainly fish, aquatic insects and crustaceans.
Sticks and twigs.	In trees or shrubs, 5-12 ft. up.	Insects, especially grasshoppers; frogs, spiders. Also ticks.
Grasses, sedges, and mosses.	6 ft. diameter mound in marshes or wet grassy meadows.	Stems, seeds, and roots of aquatic plants.
Twigs, weeds, grasses, lined with down.	On dry ground near water, often on small island.	Pondweeds, grasses; seeds of wheat, barley, sedges.
Reeds and grasses, lined with down.	On ground among high grass or reeds; usually near water.	Pondweeds, wild rice and other seeds; aquatic insects.
Grasses, weeds, leaves; feather lining.	Usually on ground in grass or brush. Sometimes far from water.	Same as Mallard.
Grasses, twigs, leaves; down-lined.	Up to 60 ft. above ground; in a hole in tree or stump.	Wild rice, pondweeds, acorns, seeds, and fruits; some insects.

Page	Name	Migration		Eggs	
		Arrive	Depart	Size (in.)	No.
31	Northern Pintail	NY M-Sept StL L-Sept SF E-Sept P Permanent Resident	WR M-Apr Tr L-Apr WR L-Apr	2.2 × 1.5 Similar to Mallard.	5-12
32	Canvasback	DC E-Nov NY M-Oct StL L-Oct SF M-Oct	WR E-Apr WR M-Apr WR L-Apr WR L-Apr	2.5 × 1.6 Olive gray or dull green.	6-10
33	Common Merganser	DC M-Nov B M-Nov StL M-Nov P Permanent Resident	WR E-Apr WR L-Apr WR M-Apr	2.5 × 1.7 Pale buff; unmarked.	6-17
34	American Coot	DC M-Oct NY E-Oct StL M-Feb SF Permanent Resident	WR E-May Tr L-Nov SR M-Nov	1.9 × 1.3 Light buff, speckled with dark brown or black.	8-12
35	Killdeer	NY E-Mar B L-Mar StL L-Feb SF Permanent Resident	SR E-Nov SR L-Oct SR L-Nov	1.5 × 1.1 Buff or darker; heavily spotted or mottled.	4
36	Common Snipe	DC M-Sept StL L-Feb SF E-Sept P Permanent Resident	Tr E-May Tr L-Nov WR E-May	1.6 × 1.2 Pale olive to brown; darker spots and specks.	4
37	Lesser Yellowlegs	DC E-Apr NY E-Apr StL E-Apr SF E-Aug	Tr M-Oct Tr E-Oct Tr E-Oct Tr E-May	1.6 × 1.1 Buffy with bold blotches of chocolate and blackish.	3-5
38	Spotted Sandpiper	DC M-Apr B E-May StL M-Apr P L-Apr	SR L-Sept SR M-Sept SR E-Oct SR M-Oct	1.3 × 0.9 White to cream; heavily marked with dark brown and black.	4
39	Least Sandpiper	DC L-Apr StL E-Apr SF E-July P E-May	Tr L-Sept Tr L-Oct WR M-May Tr L-Sept	1.2 × 0.8 Pale brown or gray; marked with brown, gray, or black.	3-4
40	Herring Gull	DC M-Sept NY L-Aug StL M-Oct SF L-Oct	WR M-May WR L-May WR L-Apr WR M-Apr	2.9 × 1.9 Variable. Whitish to gray or brown; brown spots and blotches.	3-4

Nests		Food
Materials	**Location**	
Straw, grass, rushes; lined with down.	On dry ground in the open.	Rushes, pondweeds, seeds of aquatic plants; molluscs and insects.
Reeds, lined with down.	On ground in reeds or rushes, near water.	Wild celery, pondweeds and other aquatic plants; some molluscs, and aquatic insects.
Leaves, grasses, moss; lined with down.	On ground; beneath bushes and between boulders; or in a hole in a tree.	Fish, crayfish, frogs, occasional aquatic insects.
Heaps of reeds, rushes, and coarse grass.	On ground near water; sometimes half afloat.	Duckweeds and other aquatic plants. Molluscs, crustaceans, and aquatic insects.
Slight depression lined with pebbles, grasses, or debris.	A hollow in ground, in pastures or fields.	Mainly insects and earthworms; small crustaceans.
Slight depression lined with grass.	On ground or on slight elevation in meadows, open marshes, or bogs.	Insects, crustaceans, worms, seeds of swamp and aquatic plants.
Slight depression with little or no lining.	On ground along shores and in marshes, often under small bush.	Small fish, snails, worms, crustaceans, and some insects.
Slight depression lined with grasses.	On ground or cavity in rocks, on sandy or rocky shores. Banks of streams and open upland fields.	Mainly insects; worms, spiders, and small crustaceans.
Slight depression, sparingly lined with grass.	On ground or rock in grassy lowlands near water. Sometimes on moist upland.	Aquatic insects, worms, and small crustaceans.
Seaweeds; marsh plants, chips, feathers, shells. Sometimes no nest.	On ground. Birds nest in colonies. Often on islands; sometimes under heavy vegetation.	Small fish, molluscs, crustaceans, insects, garbage, blueberries.

Page	Name	Migration		Eggs	
		Arrive	Depart	Size (in.)	No.
41	Common Tern	DC M-Apr NY L-Apr B E-May SF L-Apr	SR E-Oct SR M-Oct SR E-Oct Tr E-Nov	1.6 × 1.2 Variable. Dull greenish white to brown; darker spots.	2-3
42	Turkey Vulture	DC Permanent Resident NY L-Mar SF E-Mar P M-Mar	SR M-Nov SR M-Nov SR L-Sept	2.8 × 1.9 Dull white or buff; irregular brown spots.	1-3
43	Osprey	DC L-Mar B L-Apr StL E-Apr SF M-Mar	SR M-Oct SR E-Oct Tr L-Oct SR M-Oct	2.5 × 1.8 Variable. Dull white to buff or light brown with brown blotches.	2-4
44	Bald Eagle	DC Permanent Resident		3.5 × 2.9 White; unmarked.	1-4
45	Cooper's Hawk	NY E-Apr B M-Apr StL M-Mar SF Permanent Resident	Tr E-Oct SR E-Oct SR L-Oct	1.9 × 1.6 Bluish or greenish white; unmarked to heavily spotted with brown.	3-6
46	Red-tailed Hawk	Permanent Resident throughout its range, except in north central states		2.6 × 1.8 Dull or creamy white; spotted brown or purple; rarely unmarked.	2-4
47	American Kestrel	Permanent Resident throughout its range, except in north central states and Canada		1.3 × 1.2 White or tinted with buff; spotted or speckled with brown.	4-7
48	Ring-necked Pheasant	Permanent Resident throughout its range		1.8 × 1.4 Buff to dark olive; occasionally greenish.	6-16
49	Ruffed Grouse	Permanent Resident throughout its range		1.5 × 1.1 Pale buff but varying in color; unmarked.	8-14
50	Northern Bobwhite	Permanent Resident throughout its range		1.2 × 1.0 White; unmarked.	10-24

Nests		Food
Materials	**Location**	
Hollow, lined with shells, to well-built mound of grass and seaweed.	On sand or bare rock, sometimes among grasses. Usually on islands.	Feeds almost wholly on small fish, but also some insects.
None.	On ground, rock ledge, or hollow log in secluded places, near water or in woods.	Carrion.
Platform of sticks; additions made from year to year.	In trees: 15-50 ft. up or on rocks. Ospreys nest along coasts.	Almost entirely fish.
Large nest of branches and sticks. Additions and repairs are made yearly.	In treetops or cliffs; 30-90 ft. up; in forested or wooded regions, near streams, lakes, or ocean.	Mostly fish; some rodents and a few birds.
Branches and twigs; often lined with bark.	Usually in trees: pines preferred, 25-65 ft. up. Rarely on ground.	Mainly wild birds and poultry; some mammals; other vertebrates and insects.
Branches and twigs; lined with grasses, weeds, dead leaves.	In tall trees, 20-80 ft. up; in forest areas or in small groves.	Mainly rodents; some reptiles and poultry.
No nest material, unless some was left by previous occupant.	In cavity of tree, cliff embankment, 7-80 ft. up; often in farms or orchards.	Largely insects, some rodents, lizards, and small birds.
Dead leaves, grass, straw.	On ground in bushy pastures, moorlands, grass, and grain fields.	Corn, wheat, barley, wild fruits, and insects.
Shallow depression, lined with leaves.	On ground, at base of tree in wooded uplands or dense thicket; under logs.	Leaves, buds, and fruits of forest plants. Occasional insects.
Grass, stems, strips of bark.	On ground in grass tangles, open fields, hedgerows.	Corn and grain. Ragweed, lespedeza, acorns, and weed seeds.

Page	Name	Migration		Eggs	
		Arrive	Depart	Size (in.)	No.
51	Rock Dove	Permanent Resident throughout its range		1.5 × 1.1 White; unmarked.	2-3
52	Mourning Dove	DC Permanent Resident NY M-Mar SR M-Nov B L-Mar SR L-Oct SF L-Mar SR M-Nov		1.1 × 0.8 White; unmarked.	2
53	Yellow-billed Cuckoo	DC E-May SR L-Sept NY E-May SR L-Sept StL L-Apr SR L-Sept SF L-May SR L-Sept		1.2 × 0.9 Light bluish green; unmarked; occasionally mottled.	2-4
54	Common Barn Owl	Permanent Resident except at northern edge of its range		1.6 × 1.2 White; unmarked.	5-11
55	Great Horned Owl	Permanent Resident throughout its range		2.3 × 1.9 Rough white; unmarked.	2-3
56	Eastern and Western Screech-Owls	Permanent Residents throughout their range		1.4 × 1.3 White; unmarked.	3-5
57	Chimney Swift	DC M-Apr SR E-Oct B L-Apr SR E-Sept StL E-Apr SR E-Oct		0.8 × 0.5 White; unmarked.	4-5
58	Whip-poor-will	DC L-Apr SR M-Sept B E-May SR M-Sept StL M-Apr SR M-Oct		1.2 × 0.8 Creamy white; spotted with brown.	2
59	Common Nighthawk	DC E-May SR L-Sept B M-May SR M-Sept StL L-Apr SR E-Oct P E-June SR L-Sept		1.2 × 0.9 Dull white; spotted with gray and brown.	2
60	Ruby-throated Hummingbird	DC L-Apr SR L-Sept NY M-May SR M-Sept StL L-Apr SR E-Oct		0.5 × 0.4 White; unmarked.	2

Nests		Food
Materials	**Location**	
Sticks, straw, and debris.	Building (30 ft. and higher), on sheltered eaves or ledge.	Corn, oats, weed seeds, farm gleanings.
Stems, straws, sometimes leaves and moss.	In trees (pines preferred) 2-45 ft. above ground; in upland, sometimes in wet lowlands.	Wheat, corn, grass, and weed seeds.
Sticks, rootlets, straws, pine needles, lichens.	In trees or thickets, 3-20 ft. up. Prefers margins of woods, orchards, or thickets.	Insects, mostly caterpillars, including hairy species.
Sometimes rubbish or debris. Usually no nest.	Tree cavities; steeples, barns. Sometimes underground in burrows or holes in embankments.	Mice, rats, gophers, and some birds.
Sometimes uses old hawk nests; sometimes none.	In large trees (preferably pines) 10-90 ft. up. Sometimes in tree hollow or even on ground.	Rabbits, squirrels, rats, wild birds and poultry.
No nest; or uses any available material.	Hollow of tree (5-50 ft. up), cranny, nook of building.	Rodents, small birds, frogs, fish, and insects.
Coarse twigs, held together by saliva of bird.	Usually near top of chimneys or rarely in barns or sheds; sometimes inside wells.	Flies, mosquitoes, and other small insects, caught in flight.
No nest construction. Uses slight depression in leaves.	On ground, usually in brushy wood margins, on well-drained land.	Moths, flying ants, and other insects caught in flight.
None. Eggs laid on bare surface.	On ground, rock, or on flat roofs of building; in open fields, pastures, or city lots.	Similar to Whip-poor-will.
Plant-down, bits of lichen outside; bound by threads of saliva and spider web.	Placed or "saddled" on branch of tree—3-50 ft. above ground.	Nectar of flowers and small insects.

Page	Name	Migration		Eggs	
		Arrive	Depart	Size (in.)	No
61	Belted Kingfisher	DC Permanent Resident B E-Apr StL L-Feb SF Permanent Resident	 SR L-Oct SR L-Nov	1.3 × 1.0 Glossy white; unmarked.	5-8
62	Red-headed Woodpecker	DC Permanent Resident NY E-May StL Permanent Resident	 Tr L-Sept	1.0 × 0.8 White; unmarked.	4-6
63	Northern Flicker	DC Permanent Resident NY M-Mar B M-Apr SF Permanent Resident	 SR L-Oct SR M-Oct	1.1 × 0.9 Glossy white; unmarked.	5-9
64	Yellow-bellied Sapsucker	DC L-Sept B M-Apr StL E-Mar SF E-Oct	WR E-May Tr L-Oct Tr M-Nov WR L-Apr	0.9 × 0.7 Glossy white; unmarked.	5-7
65	Downy Woodpecker	Permanent Resident throughout its range		0.8 × 0.6 White; unmarked.	4-6
66	Eastern Kingbird	DC L-Apr NY E-May StL L-Apr P M-May	SR M-Sept SR E-Sept SR L-Sept SR M-Sept	1.0 × 0.7 Creamy white, spotted with brown.	3-4
67	Great Crested Flycatcher	DC E-May B M-May StL L-Apr	SR M-Sept SR E-Sept SR M-Sept	0.9 × 0.7 Creamy, streaked with brown.	3-6
68	Eastern Phoebe	DC M-Mar NY M-Mar StL M-Mar	SR L-Oct SR M-Oct SR L-Oct	0.8 × 0.6 White; occasionally spotted with brown.	4-5
69	Least Flycatcher	DC E-May B E-May StL E-May	Tr L-Sept SR E-Sept Tr E-Oct	0.6 × 0.5 White; unmarked.	3-4
70	Horned Lark	Permanent Resident in the United States		0.8 × 0.6 Dull white; speckled with brown or purple.	3-5

Nests		Food
Materials	**Location**	
Nest lined with fish-bones and scales, leaves, grass.	At end of burrow in bank or bluff. Usually not more than 10 ft. up. Usually near water.	Mainly fish; some crustaceans and frogs.
A gourd-shaped hole, padded with chips.	Excavations in trees, posts, poles: 5-80 ft. up.	Beetles, ants, other insects. Acorns, other wild fruits and seeds.
Hole, padded with chips.	Cavity 10-24 in. deep in trees, snags, poles: 6 in.-60 ft. up.	Ants, beetles, and other insects. Wild fruits and seeds.
Hole, lined with chips.	Cavity in dead or live tree 8-40 ft. up; in woods or orchards.	Ants, beetles, other insects and their eggs. Wood and sap; wild fruits.
Gourd-shaped excavation: 6-10 in. deep.	In dead limb 5-50 ft. up; woodlands, orchards.	Ants and boring insects, spiders, snails. Some fruits and seeds.
Rootlets, grass, twine, hair, wool. Lined with fine grass, moss.	On horizontal limb of tree; bushes, eaves, fence rails; bridges: 2-60 ft. up.	Bees, ants, grasshoppers, beetles, etc. Also some wild fruits.
Twigs, grass, leaves, moss, feathers, and usually a cast-off snakeskin.	Cavity in dead limb or post. Sometimes buildings; 3-70 ft. up.	Moths, grasshoppers, other flying insects. Occasional fruits.
Of mud, covered with moss and dead leaves, lined with grass rootlets, moss, feathers.	In shelter of undercut banks, tree roots, culverts, eaves, or inside farm buildings; 1-20 ft up.	Flying insects: beetles, flies, moths, etc. Some wild fruit; few seeds.
Grasses, bark fibers, lined with feathers and other soft materials.	Fork of tree or upright twigs: 2-60 ft. up. Usually along wood margins.	Small insects: flies, mosquitoes, moths, beetles.
Depression, loosely filled with grass, fibers, feathers.	On ground, in cultivated fields, sand dunes, or barren islands; in cover of grass and moss.	Mixed diet of insects and (in winter) seeds of weeds and grasses.

Page	Name	Migration		Eggs	
		Arrive	**Depart**	**Size (in.)**	**No**
71	Purple Martin	DC L-Mar NY M-Apr StL L-Mar	SR E-Sept Tr L-Aug SR M-Sept	1.0 × 0.7 White; unmarked.	4-
72	Tree Swallow	DC L-Mar B M-Apr StL M-Mar SF E-Mar	Tr M-Oct SR M-Sept SR L-Oct SR L-Oct	0.7 × 0.6 White; unmarked.	4-
73	Barn Swallow	NY E-Apr StL E-Apr SF L-Mar P M-Apr	SR L-Sept SR L-Oct SR M-Oct SR M-Sept	0.8 × 0.5 White, spotted with brown.	3-
74	Black-billed Magpie	Permanent Resident throughout its range		1.3 × 0.9 Grayish, heavily marked with brown.	4-
75	American Crow	Permanent Resident except in Canada		1.6 × 1.2 Variable. Pale greenish or bluish, spotted or blotched with brown.	3-
76	Blue Jay	Permanent Resident throughout its range but irregular in winter in the north		1.1 × 0.9 Greenish to olive, spotted with brown.	4-
77	White-breasted Nuthatch	Permanent Resident throughout its range		0.8 × 0.6 White, rarely pinkish speckled or spotted with brown.	5-
78	Black-capped Chickadee	Permanent Resident throughout its range		0.6 × 0.5 White, finely spotted with brown.	5-
79	Tufted Titmouse	Permanent Resident throughout its range		0.7 × 0.6 White to buff; speckled with grayish brown.	5-
80	Brown Creeper	DC E-Oct NY L-Sept StL L-Sept SF Permanent Resident	WR L-Apr WR E-May WR L-Apr	0.6 × 0.5 White, speckled with brown.	5-

Nests		Food
Materials	**Location**	
Leaves, grass, straw, twigs.	In cavities of trees, holes in cliffs: 3-30 ft. high. Frequently uses multi-celled birdhouses.	Flying insects: flies, bees, beetles, flying ants, moths.
Grass, lining of feathers.	Hollows and cavities in trees, woodpecker holes, crevices in buildings; also birdhouses; 2-50 ft. up.	Flies, moths, bees, beetles and other flying insects. Uses bayberries as a winter food.
Mud reinforced with plant material. Lined with feathers.	Commonly in barns, out-buildings, porches; 5-20 ft. up. Nest adheres to an upright surface.	Entirely flying insects: flies, bees, ants, beetles.
Large nest of sticks and mud; lining of rootlets or horsehair.	In bushes and trees: 8-30 ft. up.	Grasshoppers; other insects, carrion, small mammals; wild and cultivated fruits.
Twigs and sticks, lined with rootlets, vines, grass.	In trees (preferably pine woods), height 10-70 ft.	Corn and other grains, weed seeds, wild fruits; grasshoppers and other insects.
Twigs and rootlets, lined with grass, feathers.	In a fork of tree: 5-50 ft. up. Prefers evergreen forests. But often in suburbs, farms, and villages.	Acorns, beechnuts, corn and other grain. Some insects, eggs, and young birds.
Grass, plant fibers, twigs, hair, and feathers.	A cavity or deserted woodpecker hole: 5-60 ft. up. Mature trees preferred.	Beetles, ants, other insects and their eggs. Also seeds in winter. Prefers sunflower seeds.
Moss, hair, feathers, grass; lined with plant down.	Cavity in rotted stump or limb, or deserted woodpecker hole; 1-50 ft. up.	Insects and their eggs, weed and tree seeds; wild fruits.
Leaves, moss, bark; lined with feathers.	Deserted woodpeckers' holes or stumps: 2-85 ft. up.	Ants, bugs, and other insects; some seeds and fruits.
Twigs, plant fibers; sometimes lined with spider web, feathers, or hair.	In trees, behind or between loose bark: 5-15 ft. up. Usually in deep woods.	Mainly insects: beetles, bugs, caterpillars, ants, insect eggs.

Page	Name	Migration			Eggs	
		Arrive	Depart		Size (in.)	No.
81	House Wren	DC M-Apr NY L-Apr StL M-Apr SF E-Mar	SR M-Oct SR E-Oct SR M-Oct SR L-Oct		0.7×0.5 Dull white, densely spot- ted with brown.	5-10
82	Ruby-crowned Kinglet	NY E-Apr B M-Apr StL E-Oct P M-Apr	Tr L-Oct Tr M-Oct Tr L-Apr SR M-Oct		0.5×0.4 White to cream. Similar to Golden-crowned King- let.	4-9
83	Golden-crowned Kinglet	DC E-Oct NY L-Sept StL L-Sept SF Permanent Resident	WR M-Apr WR M-Apr WR L-Apr		0.6×0.4 White to cream; spotted with pale brown.	5-10
84	Blue-gray Gnatcatcher	DC M-Apr NY L-Apr StL L-Mar SF Permanent Resident	SR M-Sept SR E-Sept SR L-Sept		0.6×0.5 White or bluish white speckled with brown.	4-5
85	Eastern Bluebird	DC Permanent Resident NY M-Mar StL L-Feb P Permanent Resident	SR M-Nov SR L-Nov		0.9×0.7 Pale blue; rarely white unmarked.	4-6
86	Wood Thrush	DC L-Apr NY E-May B M-May StL L-Apr	SR M-Oct SR E-Oct SR M-Sept SR E-Oct		1.1×0.8 Bright greenish blue; un- marked.	3-5
87	Hermit Thrush	DC M-Oct NY E-Apr B M-Apr SF Permanent Resident	WR E-May SR M-Nov SR E-Nov		0.9×0.7 Greenish blue; un- marked.	3-4
88	American Robin	DC Permanent Resident NY E-Mar StL Permanent Resident SF Permanent Resident	SR M-Nov		1.2×0.8 Greenish blue; rarely spotted.	3-5
89	Gray Catbird	DC L-Apr NY E-May StL L-Apr	SR L-Oct SR E-Oct SR M-Oct		0.9×0.7 Deep greenish blue o bluish green; unmarked.	4-6
90	Northern Mockingbird	DC Permanent Resident StL Permanent Resident SF Permanent Resident			1.0×0.8 Greenish to blue; spotted brown, mostly at large end.	3-6

Nests		Food
Materials	**Location**	
Twigs, stems, grasses, lined with feathers, hair.	A cavity in hollow tree: 5-60 ft. up. Woodlands, farmyards, and in cities. Bird boxes commonly used.	Small insects: bugs, beetles, caterpillars, etc.
Plant down, covered by mosses and lichens. Bound with plant fibers.	In conifers, often saddled on a limb; 5-50 ft. up.	Ants, plant lice, scale insects, and insect eggs. Occasional use of wild fruits.
Green mosses, lined with fine inner bark, black rootlets, and feathers.	In coniferous trees, partly suspended from twigs: 4-60 ft. up.	Insects: flies, beetles, plant lice; insect eggs.
Tendrils, fine bark, and grasses. Firmly woven and covered with lichens.	On a branch or in a crotch in tree near water; 10-70 ft. up.	Mainly small insects: beetles, flies, caterpillars, moths.
Grasses, rootlets, hair, and some feathers.	In hollow trees, deserted woodpecker holes, and birdhouses; 3-30 ft. up.	Many insects, including beetles, weevils, and grasshoppers. Also holly, dogwood, and other wild fruits.
Leaves, rootlets, fine twigs. Firmly woven, with inner wall of mud.	Usually in saplings in woods; 3-40 ft. up.	Beetles, ants, caterpillars, and other insects. Some wild fruits and weed seeds.
Moss, grasses, leaves. Lined with rootlets and pine needles.	On or near ground in pine or hemlock woods.	Food similar to Wood Thrush.
Mud wall and bottom, reinforced with grass, twine, twigs. Lined with grass.	In tree crotch or among branches, 5-70 ft. up. In woods or open country. On buildings, in rural areas.	Garden and field insects, worms; cultivated and wild fruits. Some seeds.
Twigs and leaves. Lined with bark shreds, rootlets.	In shrubbery, thicket; 1-10 ft. and rarely 25 ft. up. Prefers dense lowlands.	Food similar to Mockingbird.
Bulky nest of coarse twigs, weed stems, shreds, string, rags.	In shrubs, thickets, vines; near houses; 1-15 ft. up, rarely higher.	Beetles, grasshoppers, and other insects; some wild fruit in season—grape and holly preferred.

Page	Name	Migration		Eggs	
		Arrive	Depart	Size (in.)	No.
91	Brown Thrasher	DC E-Apr NY L-Apr B L-Apr StL M-Mar	SR M-Oct SR M-Oct SR M-Sept SR M-Nov	1.1×0.8 3-6 Grayish or greenish white; thickly spotted with brown.	
92	Cedar Waxwing	DC E-Sept NY M-May StL L-Sept P Permanent Resident	WR E-June SR M-Nov WR M-June	0.9×0.6 3-5 Grayish blue; speckled brown or black, mostly at large end.	
93	Loggerhead Shrike	NY E-Aug B M-Mar StL Permanent Resident SF Permanent Resident	Tr L-Oct Tr L-Oct	1.0×0.8 3-5 Dull white; spotted and blotched with light brown.	
94	European Starling	Permanent Resident throughout its range, except in extreme North		1.2×0.9 4-6 Whitish or pale blue; un- marked.	
96	Yellow Warbler	DC L-Apr NY E-May StL L-Apr SF M-Apr	SR M-Sept SR L-Aug SR M-Sept SR L-Sept	0.7×0.5 4-5 Pale bluish white; brown spots forming ring at larger end.	
96	Black-and-white Warbler	DC M-Apr NY L-Apr StL M-Apr	SR E-Oct SR M-Sept SR L-Sept	0.7×0.5 4-5 Greenish white to buff; spotted and blotched with brown.	
96	Black-throated Blue Warbler	DC E-May NY E-May B M-May StL E-May	Tr E-Oct Tr L-Sept Tr M-Sept Tr M-Sept	0.7×0.5 3-5 Creamy white; speckled with brown and laven- der, mostly at larger end.	
98	Common Yellowthroat	DC L-Apr NY E-May StL E-Apr SF Permanent Resident	SR M-Oct SR M-Oct SR E-Oct	0.7×0.5 3-5 Creamy white; speckled with brown and black; chiefly at large end.	
98	Ovenbird	DC L-Apr NY M-May StL L-Apr	SR E-Oct SR M-Sept SR E-Oct	0.8×0.6 4-6 White, spotted with brown, especially at larger end.	
98	Northern Waterthrush	DC L-Apr B M-May StL L-Apr	Tr L-Sept Tr E-Sept Tr L-Sept	0.8×0.6 4-5 White to creamy; spotted with brown and gray.	

Nests		Food
Materials	**Location**	
Bulky nest of coarse twigs, weed stalks, leaves. Lined with rootlets, grass.	In bushes, vines, brush, and low trees; 0-12 ft. up.	Beetles, grasshoppers, caterpillars, etc. Also some acorns and wild fruit.
Bulky nest of bark, leaves, grasses, rootlets, moss, and sometimes mud.	Often in fruit and shade trees; 5-50 ft. up.	Wild and cultivated fruits: grapes, dogwood, hawthorn, cherries; some insects.
Strips of bark, small twigs, and vegetable fibers; lined with grasses.	In thorny hedges or low trees; 5-20 ft. up.	Insects; grasshoppers, beetles; some small rodents and birds.
Large, poorly built nest of grasses and twigs.	In hollow of tree or crevice of building; 3-40 ft. up. Uses bird boxes.	Beetles, grasshoppers, and other insects; wild and cultivated fruits and grain.
Fine grasses and fibers; lined with plant down, fine grass, some hair.	In shrubs and trees; 3-8 ft. up. Rarely 40 ft. Fields and orchards, near water.	Caterpillars, weevils, and other small insects. Slight amount of plant food.
Strips of fine bark, grasses; lined with rootlets or hairs.	On ground, at base of trees, logs, or rocks.	Plant lice, caterpillars, beetles, scale and other insects.
Bark, fine grasses, pine needles. Lining of black rootlets.	In heavy undergrowth of dense woods; 1-10 ft. up.	Mainly insects: caterpillars, small beetles, plant lice, etc.
Bark, coarse grasses, dead leaves. Lined with fine grass tendrils.	On or near ground. Usually in clump of grass, in moist location.	Insects: cankerworms, weevils, leafhoppers, caterpillars, etc.
Bulky, covered nest. Entrance at one side. Of leaves, coarse grasses, and rootlets.	On leaf-covered ground in open woods.	Beetles, grasshoppers, and other ground insects. Worms and spiders.
Moss, lined with tendrils and fine rootlets.	On ground in a mossy bank or under roots of fallen tree.	Insects: beetles, bugs, caterpillars, leafhoppers, and spiders.

Page	Name	Migration		Eggs	
		Arrive	Depart	Size (in.)	No.
100	Yellow-rumped Warbler	DC L-Sept NY L-Sept StL M-Sept SF L-Sept	WR M-May WR E-May WR M-May WR L-Apr	0.7 × 0.5 4-5 White, speckled with brown; often forming ring at larger end.	
100	American Redstart	DC L-Apr B E-May StL M-Apr	SR E-Oct SR M-Sept SR L-Sept	0.7 × 0.5 4-5 Bluish white; brown spots occasionally ringing large end.	
100	Wilson's Warbler	DC E-May NY M-May StL E-May SF L-Mar	Tr L-Sept Tr M-Sept Tr M-Sept SR L-Sept	0.7 × 0.5 4-5 White or pinkish; brown spots forming ring at larger end.	
102	Red-eyed Vireo	DC E-May B M-May StL M-Apr P E-May	SR E-Oct SR M-Sept SR E-Oct SR L-Sept	0.9 × 0.6 3-4 White, sparsely speckled with brown or black.	
103	Scarlet Tanager	DC L-Apr B M-May StL L-Apr	SR E-Oct SR M-Sept SR E-Oct	0.9 × 0.7 3-4 Pale greenish or bluish; speckled brown at larger end.	
104	Northern Cardinal	Permanent Resident		1.0 × 0.7 3-4 Pale bluish white; finely spotted with reddish brown.	
105	Rose-breasted Grosbeak	DC E-May NY M-May StL L-Apr	Tr E-Oct SR M-Sept SR E-Oct	0.9 × 0.7 4-5 Pale blue; spotted with brown.	
106	Indigo Bunting	DC L-Apr B M-May StL L-Apr	SR E-Oct SR M-Sept SR L-Oct	0.7 × 0.6 3-4 Pale bluish white; unmarked.	
107	Eastern Towhee	NY M-Apr B L-Apr StL E-Mar	SR E-Oct SR E-Oct SR L-Nov	1.0 × 0.7 4-5 White or pinkish; brown specks at large end.	
108	Canyon Towhee	Permanent Resident		1.0 × 0.7 3-4 Variable; bluish marked with purple and black.	

Nests		Food
Materials	**Location**	
Plant fibers; lining of grasses.	Coniferous trees in heavy woods; 5-40 ft. up.	Mainly common insects, but takes poison ivy, bayberry, and other fruits in winter.
Bark, leafstalks, plant down. Firmly woven and lined with rootlets.	Usually in the crotch of a sapling; 3-30 ft. above ground, rarely higher.	Small insects: flies, beetles, moths, leafhoppers, etc.
Ball of grass and moss wrapped in leaves. Lined with fine rootlets.	On ground among bushes in swampy land.	Small insects, similar to other warblers. Makes slight use of plant food.
Strips of bark, paper, plant down. Firmly and smoothly woven. Lined with bark and tendrils.	Suspended from a forked branch; 3-75 ft. up.	Caterpillars, moths, bugs, beetles, and other insects; small amount of wild fruit.
Fine twigs and weeds. Lined with vine tendrils and stems.	On horizontal limb, often near its end; 10-70 ft. up.	Mainly insects: ants, beetles, moths, caterpillars. Dogwood, blackberry, and other wild fruits.
Twigs, rootlets, strips of bark. Lined with grasses and rootlets.	In thick bushes or vines; 2-10 ft. up. Rarely up to 30 ft.	Grape, holly, blackberry; wild seeds and a good many kinds of insects.
Loose nest of fine twigs, weeds, rootlets.	In trees or bushes; 5-20 ft. up.	Insects, including beetles, caterpillars, ants, bees. Wild fruits when available.
Grasses, bits of dead leaves, bark; lined with fine grass, rootlets, hairs.	In crotch of bush or sapling; 1-10 ft. up. Rarely as high as 20 ft.	Diet mixed: caterpillars and other insects; some wild fruits, weed seeds.
Dead leaves and bark; lined with fine grasses.	Usually on ground, sometimes in bushes or saplings; 0-10 ft. up.	Wild fruits and weed seeds. Insects, worms, and spiders.
Grasses, weeds, and twigs. Lined with rootlets.	On ground or in low bushes. Less than 10 ft. up.	Oats and barley; weed seeds, caterpillars and other insects.

Page	Name	Migration		Eggs	
		Arrive	Depart	Size (in.)	No.
110	Field Sparrow	NY M-Apr B M-Apr StL E-Mar	SR L-Oct SR M-Oct SR L-Nov	0.7 × 0.5 White to pale blue or green; speckled with brown.	3-5
110	American Tree Sparrow	NY M-Nov B L-Oct StL M-Nov P L-Oct	WR L-Mar WR E-Apr WR L-Mar WR M-Mar	0.8 × 0.6 Pale greenish or bluish green; speckled with light brown.	4-5
110	Vesper Sparrow	DC E-Apr B M-Apr StL M-Mar P E-Apr	SR L-Oct SR M-Oct Tr E-Nov SR M-Sept	0.9 × 0.6 Dull white; thickly spotted with brown.	4-5
112	Chipping Sparrow	DC L-Mar B M-Apr StL L-Mar SF M-Apr	SR E-Nov SR M-Oct SR L-Oct SR M-Oct	0.7 × 0.5 Greenish blue; speckled with brown, mostly at larger end.	4-5
112	White-crowned Sparrow	DC E-May NY M-May StL M-Apr SF Permanent Resident	Tr M-Nov Tr L-Oct Tr L-Nov	0.9 × 0.6 Bluish and greenish white, spotted with brown.	4-5
112	White-throated Sparrow	DC L-Sept NY L-Sept StL E-Oct	WR M-May Tr M-May Tr M-May	0.8 × 0.6 White to bluish; speckled and blotched with reddish brown.	4-5
114	Song Sparrow	Permanent Resident over much of its range		0.8 × 0.6 Variable. White or greenish; spotted and speckled with brown.	4-5
114	Swamp Sparrow	DC E-Oct B M-Apr StL E-Oct	WR E-May SR M-Oct WR L-Apr	0.8 × 0.6 Bluish white; spotted or blotched with brown.	4-5
114	Fox Sparrow	DC L-Oct NY M-Oct StL E-Oct SF E-Oct	Tr E-Apr Tr M-Apr Tr M-Apr WR L-Apr	0.8 × 0.6 Greenish white; spotted with dull brown.	4-5
116	Dark-eyed Junco	DC E-Oct NY L-Sept StL E-Oct P E-Oct	WR E-May WR E-May WR L-Apr WR M-Mar	0.8 × 0.6 Pale bluish white; brown spots may form ring at larger end.	4-5

Nests		Food
Materials	Location	
Coarse grasses, weeds, rootlets. Lined with fine grass and hairs.	On ground or low bushes (10 ft. or less) in fields, overgrown pastures.	Similar to American Tree Sparrow, with some use of grain.
Grasses, rootlets, and hair.	On ground or in stunted conifers near timberline; near water.	Largely weed seeds; crabgrass, pigweed, sedge, etc. Some insects eaten.
Coarse grass. Lined with finer grasses, rootlets, hairs.	On ground in dry upland fields; along dry roadsides.	Weed seeds of many kinds; some grain, and various insects.
Grasses, fine twigs, rootlets. Thickly lined with hair.	In trees or bushes; in shrubbery near houses; 3-35 ft. up. Rarely on ground.	Weed seeds, oats, and timothy; leafhoppers and other common insects.
Grasses, moss, and rootlets. Lined with hair.	Usually on ground or in clump of grass in woods or thickets.	Ragweed, pigweed, knotweed, and other weed seeds; some grain and a number of kinds of insects.
Grasses, rootlets, moss, strips of bark. Lined with finer grasses.	Usually on ground in hedgerows and woodland undergrowth.	Food very similar to that of White-crowned Sparrow.
Nest of grasses and rootlets. Lined with fine grasses and hair.	On ground or in low bushes; in grass thickets or saplings. Up to 8 ft.; rarely 15 ft.	Food similar to that of Swamp Sparrow.
Coarse grasses, rootlets, dead leaves. Lined with finer grasses and sometimes hair.	On or close to ground; in grasses in wet meadows, marshes or swamps.	Seeds of weeds and grasses. Beetles, caterpillars, and other insects.
Coarse grasses. Lined with finer grasses, hair, mosses, feathers.	On ground or in low bushes; coniferous forests or alder thickets preferred.	Weed seeds, wild fruits, some grain, millipedes, and various insects.
Grasses, moss, and rootlets. Lined with fine grass and hair.	On or very near ground in fallen tree, logs, upturned roots; under overhanging banks, along wood roads.	Ragweed, crabgrass, and other weed seeds. Some caterpillars and other insects.

Page	Name	Migration		Eggs	
		Arrive	Depart	Size (in.)	No.
117	Eastern Meadowlark	DC Permanent Resident NY M-Mar SR L-Oct B L-Mar SR L-Oct StL Permanent Resident		1.1 × 0.8 3-7 White; completely spotted and speckled with brown.	
118	Bobolink	DC E-May Tr L-Sept B M-May SR M-Sept StL E-May Tr L-May P L-May SR M-Sept		0.9 × 0.6 4-7 Dull white; spotted and blotched with brown and gray.	
119	Red-winged Blackbird	DC M-Feb SR M-Nov NY M-Mar SR L-Oct StL E-Mar SR E-Nov SF Permanent Resident		1.0 × 0.7 3-5 Bluish white; irregular spots and streaks of purple and black.	
120	Brewer's Blackbird	StL M-Mar Tr E-Apr SF Permanent Resident P Permanent Resident		1.0 × 0.8 4-7 Dull white; almost entirely spotted with brown and black.	
121	Common Grackle	DC M-Feb SR L-Nov NY E-Mar SR E-Nov StL Permanent Resident		1.2 × 0.8 3-7 Bluish white; speckled and spotted dark brown to black.	
122	Brown-headed Cowbird	DC E-Mar SR E-Nov NY M-Mar SR M-Oct StL E-Mar SR L-Nov P E-May SR L-Sept		0.9 × 0.7 4-5 White or bluish; heavily speckled with gray or brown.	
123	Baltimore Oriole	DC L-Apr Tr L-Sept NY M-May SR E-Sept StL M-Apr SR E-Sept		0.9 × 0.6 4-6 White; irregular streaks and blotches of brown and black.	
124	Purple Finch	DC E-Oct WR E-May NY L-Mar Tr E-Nov StL E-Oct WR L-Apr SF Permanent Resident		0.8 × 0.6 4-6 Blue; spotted and speckled with brown at larger end.	
125	House Finch	Permanent Resident		0.8 × 0.6 3-5 Pale blue, nearly white; thinly speckled with black.	
126	American Goldfinch	Permanent Resident		0.7 × 0.5 3-6 Pale bluish white; unmarked.	
127	House Sparrow	Permanent Resident throughout its range		0.9 × 0.6 4-7 White to dull brown; speckled with brown.	

Nests		Food
Materials	**Location**	
Grasses and weeds; often arched over.	Usually on ground in grassy fields or meadows.	Grain and wild grass seeds, wild fruits, grasshoppers, and other insects.
Nest of grasses, weed stems, and rootlets.	On ground in the tall meadow grasses.	Wild rice, cultivated grains, weed seeds, caterpillars and other insects.
Coarse grasses and weeds. Lined with finer grass and rootlets.	Attached to low bushes, reeds; usually in swamps. Usually less than 15 ft. up.	Weed and marsh plant seeds; grain; some fruit and insects in season.
Twigs and coarse grass. Lined with finer grass.	On ground or in shrubs or coniferous trees; 0-10 ft. up.	Oats and other grain, weed seeds, some insects.
Bulky, but compact. Of mud and coarse grasses; lined with finer grasses.	Nests in colonies, most often in coniferous trees; sometimes in bushes; 5-80 ft. up.	Grain and weed seeds. Some wild fruit; beetles, grasshoppers, crickets, etc.
None added.	Eggs laid in nests of other birds. Usually 1 or 2 in any one nest.	Grain and weed seeds. Grasshoppers and other insects.
Grasses, plant fibers, hair, string, etc. Firmly interwoven.	Hanging from end of branches in shade or fruit trees; 10-90 ft. up.	Caterpillars, beetles, and other insects; wild and some cultivated fruits.
Twigs, grasses, and rootlets. Thickly lined with hairs.	Woods, in pine and spruce trees; 5-60 ft. up.	Tree seeds and wild fruits. Some insects.
Rootlets and grasses. Lined with horsehair.	Trees, bushes, and vines; 5-20 ft. above ground. Often on or near buildings.	Weed seeds, tree seeds, plant lice and other insects.
Fine grasses, bark, moss; thickly lined with thistledown.	In trees or bushes; 5-35 ft. up.	Mainly weed seeds, grain, and wild fruit. Occasional plant lice and caterpillars.
Of any available material: string, straw, twigs, paper, etc.	In any available place: in buildings, structures, eaves; over 5 ft. up.	Corn, oats, wheat, and other grain; weed seeds; some insects during spring and summer.

AIDS FOR BIRDING

BOOKS

Robbins, Chandler S., B. Bruun, and H. S. Zim, *Birds of North America, A Guide to Field Identification*. St. Martin's Press, New York, rev. ed. 2001.
Latimer, J. P., and Karen Stray Nolting, *Backyard Birds*. 1999, *Birds of Prey*. 1999; *Shorebirds*. 1999; *Songbirds*. 2000. All Houghton Mifflin, Boston.
Coe, James, *Eastern Birds*. St. Martin's Press, New York, rev. ed. 2001.
Peterson, R. T., *A Field Guide to the Birds: A Completely New Guide to All the Birds of Eastern and Central North America*. rev. ed. 1998; *A Field Guide to Western Birds*. rev. ed. 1990. Both Houghton Mifflin, Boston.
National Geographic Society, *National Geographic Field Guide to the Birds of North America: Revised and Updated*. Washington, DC, 1999.
Kaufman, Kenn, *Lives of North American Birds*. Houghton Mifflin, Boston, 1996.
Terres, John K., *The Audubon Society Encyclopedia of North American Birds*. Knopf, New York, 1980.

MAGAZINES

WildBird, P. O. Box 57347, Boulder, CO 80323-7347, www.animalnetwork.com.
Bird Times, 7-L Dundas Circle, Greensboro, NC 27499-0765.
Bird Watcher's Digest, P. O. Box 110, Marietta, OH 45750-9962.
Birder's World, P. O. Box 1612, Waukesha, WI 53187-9950.

WEBSITES

The web is full of interesting information about birds and birding. Some good places to start are:

http://birdsource.cornell.edu/—Cornell Lab. Of Ornithology
http://www.birdwatching.com/index.html
http://www-stat.wharton.upenn.edu/~siler/birdlinks.html
http://www.birding.com/
http://www.pwrc.usgs.gov/—USGS Patuxent Wildlife Research Center

MUSEUMS AND ZOOS are good places for finding additional information about birds.

Cambridge, MA: Museum of Comparative Zoology, Harvard University
Chicago, IL: Field Museum of Natural History; Brookfield Zoo
Los Angeles, CA: Los Angeles Zoo; Los Angeles County Museum
Milwaukee, WI: Milwaukee County Zoo
New York, NY: American Museum of Natural History; Bronx Zoo
San Antonio, TX: San Antonio Zoo
San Diego, CA: San Diego Zoo; San Diego Wild Animal Park
St. Louis, MO: St. Louis Zoo
Tucson, AZ: Arizona-Sonora Desert Museum
Washington, DC: National Museum of Natural History; National Zoological Park

PLACES FOR STUDYING BIRDS

These National Wildlife Refuges (NWR), National Parks (NP), and other areas are famous for their number and variety of birds.

Greater Roadrunner (22 in.), a long-tailed desert bird, rarely flies.

UNITED STATES

Alabama: Choctaw NWR, Jackson. **Alaska:** Denali NP. **Arizona:** Madera Canyon, Tucson; Ramsey Canyon, Huachuca Mountains. **Arkansas:** White River NWR, DeWitt; Ouachita NF. **California:** Tule-Klamath Basin, Tulelake; Yosemite NP; Salton Sea; Bodega Bay. **Colorado:** Rocky Mt. NP. **Connecticut:** Audubon Nature Center, Greenwich. **Delaware:** Bombay Hook NWR, Smyrna. **Florida:** Everglades NP, Homestead; J. N. "Ding" Darling NWR, Sanibel. **Georgia:** Okefenokee NWR, Folkston. **Hawaii:** James C. Campbell NWR. **Idaho:** Grays Lake NWR, Wayan. **Illinois:** Shawnee NF. **Indiana:** Muscatatuck NWR. **Iowa:** De Soto NWR, Blair. **Kansas:** Cheyenne Bottoms, Great Bend. **Kentucky:** Daniel Boone NF. **Louisiana:** Sabine NWR, Hackberry. **Maine:** Acadia NP, Bar Harbor. **Maryland:** Ocean City. **Massachusetts:** Cape Cod National Seashore. **Michigan:** Seney NWR, Seney. **Minnesota:** Crane Meadows NWR, Little Falls. **Mississippi:** Mississippi Sandhill Crane NWR, Gautier. **Missouri:** Swan Lake NWR, Mendon. **Montana:** Medicine Lake NWR, Medicine Lake. **Nebraska:** Platte River. **Nevada:** Ruby Lake NWR, Ruby Valley. **New Hampshire:** Great Bay NWR, Newington. **New Jersey:** Cape May NWR, Cape May; Edwin B. Forsyth NWR, Oceanville. **New Mexico:** Bitter Lake NWR, Roswell; Bosque del Apache, Socorro. **New York:** Central Park, Manhattan; Jamaica Bay Wildlife Refuge, Queens. **North Carolina:** Mattamuskeet NWR, Swan Quarter. **North Dakota:** Theodore Roosevelt NP, Medora. **Ohio:** Ottawa NWR, Oak Harbor. **Oklahoma:** Wichita Mts. NWR. **Oregon:** Umatilla NWR, Umatilla. **Pennsylvania:** Hawk Mtn. Sanctuary, Kempton. **Rhode Island:** Sakonnet Pt., Little Compton. **South Carolina:** Cape Romain NWR, Mt. Pleasant. **South Dakota:** Sand Lake NWR, Columbia. **Tennessee:** Great Smoky NP, Gatlinburg. **Texas:** Aransas/Matagorda Island NWR, Austwell; Laguna Atascosa NWR, Rio Honda. **Utah:** Bear River Migratory Bird Refuge, Brigham City. **Vermont:** Missisquoi NWR, Swanton. **Virginia:** Back Bay NWR, Virginia Beach; Great Dismal Swamp NWR, Suffolk. **Washington:** Willapa NWR, Ilwaco; Olympic NP. **West Virginia:** Ohio River Islands NWR, Parkersburg. **Wisconsin:** Horicon NWR, Mayville. **Wyoming:** Yellowstone NP.

CANADA

Alberta: Banff NP; Elk Island NP, Edmonton. **British Columbia:** Victoria Island; Garibaldi Prov. Park. **Manitoba:** Churchill; Riding Mt. NP. **New Brunswick:** Grand Manan, Bay of Fundy. **Ontario:** Algonquin Provincial Pk.; Pt. Pelee NP. **Quebec:** Bonaventure Island.

SCIENTIFIC NAMES

This list of scientific names is included because the common names for birds sometimes differ from place to place or time to time. The list includes all the birds illustrated in this book. It follows the standard practice of listing the name of the genus first and the species second. The page number for each illustration is listed in bold type.

16 Lewis's Woodpecker: Melanerpes lewis
Downy Woodpecker: Picoides pubescens
Pine Siskin: Carduelis pinus
18 Cyanocitta stelleri
19 Icteria virens
21 Gavia immer
22 Podilymbus podiceps
23 Ardea herodias
24 Butorides virescens
25 Bubulcus ibis
26 Cygnus columbianus
27 Branta canadensis
28 Anas platyrhynchos
29 Anas rubripes
30 Aix sponsa
31 Anas acuta
32 Aythya valisineria
33 Mergus merganser
34 Fulica americana
35 Charadrius vociferus
36 Gallinago gallinago
37 Tringa flavipes
38 Actitis macularia
39 Calidris minutilla
40 Larus argentatus
41 Sterna hirundo
42 Turkey: Cathartes aura
Black: Coragyps atratus
43 Pandion haliaetus
44 Haliaeetus leucocephalus
45 Accipiter cooperii

46 Buteo jamaicensis
47 Falco sparverius
48 Phasianus colchicus
49 Bonasa umbellus
50 Colinus virginianus
51 Columba livia
52 Zenaida macroura
53 Coccyzus americanus
54 Tyto alba
55 Bubo virginianus
56 Western: Otus kennicottii
Eastern: Otus asio
57 Chaetura pelagica
58 Caprimulgus vociferus
59 Chordeiles minor
60 Archilochus colubris
61 Ceryle alcyon
62 Melanerpes erythrocephalus
63 Colaptes auratus
64 Sphyrapicus varius
65 Picoides pubescens
66 Tyrannus tyrannus
67 Myiarchus crinitus
68 Sayornis phoebe
69 Empidonax minimus
70 Eremophila alpestris
71 Progne subis
72 Tachycineta bicolor
73 Hirundo rustica
74 Pica hudsonia
75 Corvus brachyrhynchos
76 Cyanocitta cristata
77 Sitta carolinensis

INDEX

Asterisks (*) indicate pages on which birds are illustrated.